Beyond Karma

TRIGUEIRINHO

Beyond Karma

A book that clarifies Destiny

Editorial Revision by:
Artur de Paula Carvalho

Shasta Association

Copyright © 2021 Jose Trigueirinho Netto

The profits generated from sales of books by Trigueirinho and his associates will be used to support the non-profit activities of the Shasti Association to disseminate their work.

Original Title in Portuguese:

ALÉM DO CARMA – Sao Paulo, Brazil: Editora Pensamento.
Copyright © 1996 by José Trigueirinho Netto

Cover photo by John David Cutrell

Illustratrions by Artur de Paula Carvalho

Translation and revision by John David Cutrell and Yatri (Frances O'Gorman, PhD)

Cataloging-in-Publication data

Trigueririnho Netto, José
Beyond Karma: A Book that Clarifies Destiny
Trigueirinho. – Mount Shasta, CA, Shasti Association 2nd edition, 2021
120 p.
ISBN: 978-1-948430-08-1
Library of Congress Control Number: 2021930540
1. Spirituality
2. Karma
3. Occult Science
I. Title.

English language rights reserved

Shasti Association
P.O. Box 318
Mt. Shasta, CA 96067-0318
editorial@shasti.org
www.shasti.org

Contents

To the Reader 7

Introduction 9

Part 1

The Law of Karma

Karma and Neutrality 15

A Law with Many Faces 19

Part 2

Karma in the Life of Human Beings

What Karma Teaches Us 27

Family Ties in the Karmic Web 35

Restoring Equilibrium and Healing through Karma 45

Part 3
Liberation from Karma

The Way out of the Labyrinth 53
Liberation by Fulfilling Broader Laws 59

Part 4
Beyond Karma

Monadic Transmutation 65
The New Genetic Code 69
Awakening of the Right Side Consciousness 75

Part 5
Karma in the Life of the Planets

Ties That Go beyond the Ages 85
The Karma of the Evolving Kingdoms on Earth 89
Governance of the Law of Karma over the Planets 97
A New Stage 101

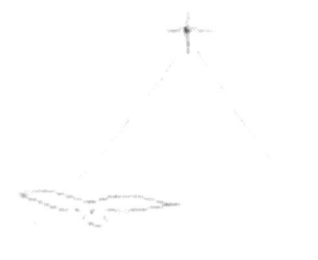

To the Reader

Let us imagine a pebble being thrown into the middle of a pond. As it splashes on the surface of the water, it stirs up concentric ripples. These ripples spread out in widening circles. As they do so, they cause other things to happen, in varying degrees and intensity, depending on what lies along their path.

Just as a pebble cast into the water stirs up ripples, everything we do on the mental, emotional and physical-etheric levels reverberates and has a ripple effect on the surrounding universe. Even when we blink, we cause a flurry in the most distant stars. Emotional and mental actions have an even stronger effect than physical ones because the energy on the levels where they take place is less condensed and the interactions are more intense. There is no movement in the world that does not give rise to new movements. The modulating power of this mechanism that links action to reaction is called the law of cause and effect, or the law of karma.

Furthermore, the consequences of a movement reflect back to its generating source in order to maintain the equilibrium of the universe, that is to say, the effects of an action return to the point of origin. This is called karmic return.

Karmic return can be positive or negative, depending on the quality of the original cause and on the transformations the impulse undergoes along its course through the Universe. In general, people have not realized this; they have not become aware of the law of karma. This is why they carelessly keep throwing pebbles into the water without giving a thought as to what will happen afterward.

If we understand the law of karma, we see that the events of our life that make up the pattern of our earthly destiny are not a punishment meted out by a pitiless God, or a whim of mere chance, but the interaction between cause and effect. The law of karma makes it possible to restore equilibrium to the imbalances that have been generated. Understanding this encourages us to simplify our lives and to avoid the conflict we normally stir up.

Although until now this material law has been basic for the evolutionary process of the Earth, human beings have always had the possibility of transcending it. This possibility is now being extended to a greater number of individuals and the entire planet is experiencing a unique transformation.

Going back to the analogy of the pebble thrown into the pond, we could say that the ripples spread mostly over the surface of the water. As the pebble sinks, the surroundings react in different ways. Likewise, the law of karma acts on the dense surface levels of existence. However, on deeper levels we are not guided by the law of karma but by what is known as the higher law of evolution or by even higher aspects of the law of equilibrium.

Many people are now being prepared to go on to higher levels of the law of evolution, to live consciously on deeper levels of being. This is the focus of the reflections presented in this book.

Trigueirinho
2003

Introduction

This book came about as a response to the need expressed by many people to become familiar with the law of karma in order to be helped in dealing with what it implies and, above all, to learn how to transcend it.

Although widely disseminated in many Eastern countries, the law of karma has rarely been taught in Western culture. Daily news and reports stressed by the media reveal that it is still practically unknown. Murders, robberies, accidents, victories, celebrations, gatherings, and rivalries — all these would be looked at differently if the law of karma were taken into account. Anyone who is familiar with karma knows that there is no such thing as coincidence, victim, culprit or reason for bewilderment, no matter what may happen.

According to the law of karma, everything grows out of what was sown in the past. Thus we can understand that impoverishment, need and hostility stem from former erroneous actions, whereas true abundance is the fruit of good works. One should also keep in mind that, depending on one's attitudes, negative situations can be avoided or redirected.

Nevertheless, although destiny is governed by the law of karma, some circumstances cannot be attributed solely to its influence, such as the cancer suffered by Sri Ramana Maharshi

(India, 1879 — 1950). The illnesses of certain spiritual teachers, or of people on the path to holiness, are outside this sphere. These ailments are often a service rendered for the sake of humanity, not a retribution for past misdeeds. In such cases they can be offered up as the hidden and silent labor of one's physical cells, which reverberates in a beneficial and purifying way on the karma of all humanity.

All the atoms that exist come from a single repository. When we incarnate, we attract a portion of these atoms to make up our cells and to form our bodies. In this way we take on a part of the general karma of the planet's atoms. Likewise, whatever purification we carry out within ourselves is reflected on this repository when the atoms are returned at the end of an incarnation.

In her writings, Saint Teresa of Ávila[1] describes how it was clear to her when some religious person under her guidance suffered an ailment for the sake of the world or, as she would say, "mortification taken on for the love of God." It was also evident when the affliction was the result of imperfections or even of a merely circumstantial malaise.

While most situations stem from reactions to past actions, some are taken on as a service to humanity. However, there are also those situations that simply occur for the greater *glory of God*. The latter are almost always incomprehensible to the rational mind. A typical example can be found in the Biblical account of the man born blind and cured by Jesus. His blindness came about through no fault of his own or of his parents, for none of them had engendered the causes for that blindness in a past life.

What is meant by something that happens for the glory of God? It is a special opportunity in which sparks from supraphysi-

---

[1] See Saint Teresa of Ávila (1515 — 1582), *The Life of Saint Teresa of Ávila By Herself*, translation by J.M. Cohen [Penguin Books: New York, USA, 1957].

cal reality can penetrate the material levels. Suffering is experienced in order for this reality to bring about healing above and beyond any law of materiality, and in this way, to manifest transcendent power and omniscience. Anyone who chooses to deepen silent reflection will find other meanings in events that happen in this world for the *glory of God*.

Furthermore, there are circumstances in our lives that may not be related to the rebalancing of past deeds, or to an offering for the purification of humanity, or even to the sublime grace[2] alluded to above. These events could be leading the way to new dimensions of our being, in preparation for what will be lived in the future. The way they happen, however, does not go against the law of karma but applies it in accordance with higher laws.

As has been stated, the law of karma is little studied in the West. However, even though not widespread, information about it has always been available. Those who begin to tread the spiritual path consciously will, in one way or another, get to know the law of karma in order to understand the events that destiny brings, and to cooperate in transforming them.

The law of karma is a basic aspect of spiritual instruction. It must be pointed out that submitting to it is merely one stage in the evolution of the human species. Once we have lived a certain stage of karma intelligently, we go on to other stages in which the soul is freed to follow broader paths not confined by the limitations of the ego.

Those who understand the teachings of the law of karma

---

[2] **Grace.** The action of supraphysical energies on material planes. Grace is the outward expression of something that has already take place in the inner world.

will find in them important keys for a harmonious way of living. Moreover, they will get a glimpse of the path that leads to areas of consciousness in which the higher law of evolution replaces this wise material law.

Many changes occur in the lives of those who take up their evolutionary process. As their consciousness expands, their lives become increasingly all-inclusive and therefore guided by more powerful and far-reaching energies. In this way they free themselves from the limited circle of merely personal affairs in order to take an active part in the infinite work of universal creation. They are uplifted to another level of beingness and creative energy can flow through them more freely.

Everyone who is open to transformation and to the realities of supraphysical worlds is receiving help intensely. These worlds are already a part of our lives on the inner planes and their pulsation can presently be detected in many hearts. The healing work that is carried out on subtle levels brings great harmony, purification and elevation.

In these times human beings are able to live various stages of evolution concurrently. This indicates that new laws are present and are being implemented in the environs of our planet. Thus, now more than ever, to understand and rise above the law of karma is within humanity's reach.

Part 1

The Law of Karma

Karma and Neutrality

The law of cause and effect, or law of karma, can be summarized in the well-known saying, "You reap what you sow." According to this law, actions, feelings and thoughts produce effects that, sooner or later, return to those who produced them. Thus, what one experiences today determines what will happen in the future. This is why some less philosophical languages have used the word destiny to translate the Sanskrit term karma, or karman. The Sanskrit term, however, includes broader meanings, such as the impulse to seek moral awakening.

Because of its precision and clarity, the law of karma is extremely simple, both to understand and to take into account in our daily life. It was one of the first laws to be given to humanity. In the Bible we can see one of its most primary aspects in the Mosaic principle, "an eye for an eye, a tooth for a tooth." An example of the more profound aspects can be found in the classic Bhagavad-Gita,[1] the epic written in ancient India, in which Prince Arjuna discovers the freedom that comes from acting without any attachment to the outcome of his deeds. The Bhagavad-Gita teaches that:

He who has abandoned all attachment to the fruit of works,

---

[1] See *The Gita*, translated by Sri Aurobindo, with comments by Shyam Sunder Jhunjhunwala [Pondicherry: Auropublications, 1974].

is ever satisfied of soul and is without dependence;
such a man, even though he engages in action, does nothing.

He has no personal hopes,
he has his heart and self under control,
he has renounced all sense of possession;
by doing actions only with the body, he does not incur sin.

Content with whatever gain may come to him,
lifted beyond the dualities, devoid of jealousy,
equal in success and failure,
he is not bound even when he acts.

(IV, 20-22)

Those who seek the spiritual path become open to manifest goodness, truth and beauty, which are to be found within themselves and in the universe. However, the highest expression of the intrinsic harmony in life requires total freedom and release from all ties that bind consciousness to matter, even positive ones. For this to take place, more than good deeds are necessary to balance negative ones: actions must be carried out with complete neutrality.

In fact, to seek liberation it is not enough to do good and thereby to sow seeds of a promising future, for this generates positive ties. Liberation comes from detachment from everything that one does, feels or thinks. This indicates an advanced state of evolution. Although surrounding conditions stir up emotional and mental entanglement in what is going on within and around them, there are people who do strive to attain liberation.

The law of karma focuses on continual progression toward harmony, especially by means of detached service to the universal good. Neutrality is the most direct way to achieve this.

Those who are no longer attached to any deed, whether positive or negative, can transcend the ties that bind them to what happens and therefore can overcome bonds with the law of karma. Jesus summed this up in the injunction: "to be in this world but not of this world."

A spider builds its universe without getting wrapped up in it. Yet, when building life on Earth, we human beings usually get involved and become attached to what we experience and create. It is as though we were locked in a room with only a tiny candle for a light. We see dimly as we go through many experiences in this beloved prison. We spin a web of personal thoughts, dreams, desires and goals. So we go on building our lives without being able to see the true design that has long been planned for us. We get tangled up in the threads of our web.

There comes a moment, however, when we, the spinner, hear a command from within: "Destroy your beloved web." Then we begin to detach ourselves, to let go of old ties and to avoid building superfluous bonds. Finally we enter the path of return to the worlds from which we, as sheer consciousness, one day departed.

A Law with Many Faces

The law of karma is but one aspect, a material one, of the more all-encompassing law of equilibrium, which governs all existence.

The law of equilibrium is everywhere — from the throbbing of tiny atoms to the pulsation of the stars. It is expressed in different ways and on different levels, but always guiding beings toward fulfillment. Up until now, spiritual teaching for earthly humanity has had to emphasize its more concrete expression, that is, the law of karma, because it has been one of the foremost directives for life on the surface of the planet.

The law of equilibrium can be perceived on various levels:

- ✧ as it governs the external existence of beings and their evolution within the sphere of planetary life, in which case it is called the law of karma;
- ✧ as it governs the interaction of beings with the life of the solar system, in which case it is called the higher law of evolution;
- ✧ as it governs the interaction of beings with cosmic life, in which case it is expressed in still purer forms.

The law of karma functions on the dense levels of the universes. From the minute single cell to the immense galaxies, everything on the level of matter is governed by the law of karma. It is an exact, perfect law that maintains equilibrium on the dense level. Within humanity the external existence of those who have not yet awakened to the spiritual law is entirely governed by the material aspects of the law of karma. The extent to which this material aspect of the law of equilibrium predominates in determining the course of one's life, will depend on the extent of one's involvement and ties with the world of matter.

The law of karma is expressed in a very specific way on Earth. It almost always takes on negative characteristics because by using free will human beings make choices based on their own needs and individual desires. Very rarely do they take into account a general need or an aspect of the Plan of Evolution. Because of this, they go on engendering more karmic debits than credits and do very little to balance out this dissonant state. Due to lack of neutrality, they keep on creating more ties.

For people in general, the law of karma is a tool for purification, a 'school' in which they learn how to use their free will. Such a precise and unfailing tool is needed to provide an accurate counterbalance for actions that are very often contrary to the higher rhythms of the cosmos.

While human beings blindly try to build their earthly existence, the law of karma watches over them like an infinitely wise master. While they devastate the planet for personal gain and heedlessly rush headlong into pleasure and gratification, pain and suffering prove to be the most adequate tools of the law of karma to teach them. This impressive method has been applied to human evolution ever since the beginning. Compulsory physical death and birth have always been part of this instruction of karma because a single incarnation would never suffice to balance out so many unwise human deeds.

The law of karma works basically on the mental, emotional and physical-etheric levels of life, whereas the higher law of evolution works on the intuitive and spiritual levels, and even purer forms of the law of equilibrium work on the monadic and divine levels.

Levels of Consciousness	Bodies and Nuclei of the Being	Law in Action
1 — Divine	Monadic regent	Purer aspects of the law of equilibrium
2 — Monadic	Monad	
3 — Spiritual	Body of Light	Higher law of evolution
4 — Intuitive	Soul	
5 — Mental	Abstract mental body and concrete mental body	Law of karma
6 — Astral	Astral (emotional) body	
7 — Physical-etheric	Physical-etheric body	

Laws in action on different levels of consciousness

Under the law of karma people believe that they are set apart from the universe. In this way one either keeps on living one's *own* processes or one adapts to the processes of others. This takes place through the various ties and links that are built progressively. By becoming attached to someone or something, one takes on the karma of the object of this attachment.

On the other hand, under the higher law of evolution human beings follow cyclical and orderly universal movements. These movements are part of the evolution of groups of souls. Thus the repetitive experiences characteristic of those who are living on the surface of life, symbolically represented by life on the surface of a material planet, no longer have to take place. The surface or outer face of a planet corresponds to its more peripheral consciousness. However, it also encompasses in its sphere a supraphysical life that corresponds to its deeper consciousness, its imperishable essence.

Some aspects of the law of karma are flexible. Whenever possible, destiny offers human beings altruistic tasks which are not aimed only at the material side of life. Such opportunities to develop beyond the concrete level are as necessary for an individual as for all humanity. They pave the way for one of the most important steps toward liberation: the detached offering up of the results of one's own actions and a fuller surrender of self. In the present times this kind of dispassion has special and widespread repercussion.

Life on Earth should pulsate translucently and manifest one of the vibratory patterns safeguarded by the solar archetype.[2] Essence and form should be unified; the human being is the link for this unification.

Neither the pain that is present in human life so as to bring about the balance of karmic return, nor obscureness, will any longer veil the sight of those who surrender themselves to this essence. These beings will become rays of shining light announcing new times.

---

[2] **Solar archetype**. The energy structure that contains patterns of perfection to be expressed by the present solar system.

The Earth is undergoing rapid transformation and the action of purifying forces will be intensified. Those who undertake the commitment to cooperate with this evolutionary transformation discover within themselves the joy of service and of self-surrender. They practice detachment, since they realize that forms are ephemeral and that essence is indestructible.

Part 2

Karma in the Life of Human Beings

What Karma Teaches Us

We know that on Earth there has always been violence and the massacre of the innocent. Members of the human kingdom, as well as of the animal, plant and mineral kingdoms, have been exploited.

Since cycles of unbalanced action and cycles of consequences stemming from that action have followed one after another without ever being resolved, the web of karma continues. It takes humanity a long time to realize that right living, with the renunciation of desire, is the direct way to liberation. The Buddha was quite explicit in this regard. Nevertheless, his teachings have had little impact on the daily life of most people over the centuries, although such teachings are indeed alive in the inner worlds.

As long as human beings understand facts from the point of view of their beliefs, or act according to their personal knowledge, they remain subject to the consequences of their actions and to the need to balance out the ensuing effects. In other words, they remain subject to the law of karma. Their deeds can contribute little to the good of the All since they are based on individual or egocentric intentions and are always in need of neutralizing reactions, which can come through other persons or through nature. Such reactions can purify, for they dismantle the unsound structures of individuals, groups and even entire nations or civilizations. However, if these are imbued with human forces, they will provoke further reactions. Thus, karmic entanglement of this humanity continues to be generated and keeps on spreading.

Nevertheless, much can be done by those who are already aware of the need to change this vicious pattern. As they take on the rhythms of the higher law of evolution, they can embody new conditions and contribute to the transformation of the face of the Earth. But, first of all, they must learn to conduct themselves in accordance with the governance of the law of karma.

We are continually building both positive and negative karma. Depending on our attitudes, we transform or free ourselves from it. Therefore, we must work with karma throughout our time on Earth.

Each of us has a basic karma that includes the date of our birth and death, absence or presence of congenital ailments, as well as significant encounters and incidents, serious accidents and other decisive events during incarnation. We all build the web of our own life within this basic karma, which exists prior to our actual physical birth. Depending on our life situations we either lighten or overburden our journey. In principle, basic karma should be fully accepted. Things can only improve after one has assented to one's karma.

In the lessons that the law of karma offers, even gifts come as tests: we must discover how to make good use of talents and assets that life gives us. When we waste available resources, whether they be material, intellectual or spiritual, we generate restrictive karma. This means these resources will be lacking either in this lifetime or in a future one, to the detriment of the assignments we are meant to fulfill.

Since everything is contained in the One Consciousness, the source of all that exists, no detail is to be overlooked in our quest for balance and harmony. All that we are, and everything that surrounds us, are to become instruments of service and be used appropriately. For example, water, electricity, food, money, transportation, work, sleep, spoken words, feelings, thoughts — nothing belongs to us any longer. Everything is seen for what it really is: an expression of this all-powerful Consciousness.

Karmic debts are brought on by humans because they regard themselves as being separated from the One Consciousness and they identify themselves with only a part of the whole and with transience. Most people have not generally been freed from the earthly conditioning of karma. They are unable to deal with two of the forces opposed to evolution: the force of desire for what is superfluous and the force of illusion that presents the physical level as the only or the most important reality. By neutralizing these two forces life can become less constrained by karma and, consequently, freer.

At a set time the inner being leaves the physical body to become discarnate. Periodically it needs to remain apart from the world of matter to synthesize its experiences and to prepare better conditions for the future, according to the karma woven by the ego during its stay on Earth. These conditions include the building of more suitable bodies for the new situations the incarnating soul will encounter.

It is mainly between incarnations that the inner and immortal being re-appraises its past actions, feelings and thoughts. If moderately evolved, it decides to balance out the disharmony generated in its most recent incarnation. The decisions that the inner being makes, however, are only clear while it remains outside of the physical body.

When reincarnating, the new mental, emotional and physical-etheric bodies have almost no conscious memory of what took place in former lives, or of the decisions made outside of the material sphere. It is in the body of the soul, which is more subtle, that this new impulse and clarity of resolution become registered in a lucid way. In most cases, when incarnating, the person is unaware of what he or she really came to do on Earth. This can be seen in the doubts many people have when making choices in life.

Thus, people rarely recognize opportunities to balance past faults. Such opportunities usually go beyond superficial human interests that are influenced by both heredity and environment. They do not readily accept occasions to be of service to others or to manifest compassion. They scorn the weakness of others and discard such occasions as being troublesome. In this way, they forgo these opportunities for growth in consciousness and the subsequent liberation.

As the soul matures it begins guiding and enlightening the personality with wisdom and compassion. This permits us to become aware of evolutionary decisions increasingly being made between incarnations. The possibility for the light of the soul to penetrate external consciousness can be perceived whenever soul contact is established. This light can increase in us when there is commitment and receptivity on the part of our external consciousness.

In the myth of Hercules, as described in our book, *Time for Inner Growth — The Myth of Hercules Today*, there is an episode in which the hero saves a young lady who was devoured by a monster. By doing so, he balances out his former deed of accidentally killing a queen. This episode contains some clear lessons about the law of karma. Hercules killed the one who had welcomed him and later on he saved someone who needed to be freed. Mature enough to begin to understand life and death, which are really one and the same, the hero was then better prepared to face new tasks.

The myth of the Labors of Hercules traces a route to be followed by those who perceive the importance of rising above the law of karma and of being freed from the unending turning of the wheel of rebirth on the surface of the Earth.

This particular Labor shows how each and every act reverberates infinitely, stirring up vibrations on all levels of consciousness. Worthy actions balance out previous dissonant ones and dissolve the karma engendered. The Labor highlights the fact that by paying karmic debts we begin to dissolve innate human antagonism. As personal karma becomes balanced, our masculine and feminine aspects also gain equilibrium, opening the way to higher evolution.

Certain basic practices, such as harmlessness and compassion, when incorporated into life, help people to free themselves from the karmic web that binds them to cycles of reincarnation.

One rarely remembers that aggressive attitudes almost always spring from insecurity. People who are aggressive usually feel that their personal values are being threatened. Only love and neutrality, and never negative reactions, can induce someone to transcend aggression. The web of negative karma can only be dissipated by action based on fraternal love and by firm self-control. In this way, one avoids getting carried away by conflicts and one does not become the cause of further adverse reactions.

To maintain this attitude one must truly aspire to everyone's growth. This prevents stirring up resentment that engenders more disharmony. The certainty that each one of us carries light and goodness within makes it possible for one to trust in the latent potential of others and to manifest peaceful attitudes. Thus, some day human relationships can become fraternal, free from the bonds and the animosity that negative experiences invariably provoke.

Those who seek to evolve should learn to be patient and to sharpen their sense of observation. At certain stages of life someone may think that, despite all efforts, no progress is being made or that nothing meaningful is happening. However, this is not so. Those who earnestly seek evolution become deeply transformed and events foreseen in their basic karma can be alleviated or averted. The date of disincarnating can be postponed, illnesses can be lightened and accidents can be halted or have their effects minimized. This occurs due to a person's newly developed higher qualities. As people make themselves more useful, their lives begin to take on new aspects and conditions. They respond to needs beyond merely personal ones and this becomes a part of their lives.

We pay a lot of attention to the negative things that happen to us, but we have no idea of the afflictions and problems that we have avoided by working consciously with our karma. For example, I knew a woman who was destined to suffer one of the most painful forms of cancer. She fulfilled the destiny of suffering that illness, but without any physical pain. As it happened, between the moment when her inner self chose this method of purification and the time when the cancer was to set in, this person carried out many charitable deeds and became aware of spiritual laws that she had formerly ignored. In this way, the process she was supposed to undergo was alleviated to the point that the end of her life was quite serene.

Great changes begin to take place when we surrender to a higher level of existence. As our state of consciousness expands, we enter a more general karma and begin to be governed by a destiny that is the interplay of various higher destinies. It is no longer our individual karma that now prevails in what happens to us, but rather the interplay of the karma of groups, nations and even of the planet. Our lives become integrated with more powerful forces and we go beyond the sphere of personal limitations.

I know of persons who were in great material need and this need was met when they began to dedicate themselves unselfishly to the spiritual path and to serve through altruistic groups. I know of others who were liberated from personal karmic ties to serve in the wider spheres, such as a country or the planet. Persons who had once been bound by basic duties and confined by family circles suddenly found themselves undergoing transformation and becoming released so that they could dedicate their time and energy to universal causes. This does not mean denying the value of duties to be fulfilled, even on the most restrictive and personal levels. Karmic debts can be adjusted and new conditions can arise, setting even indispensable persons free to take on greater tasks.

Cooperation is of great significance. Universal service is carried out by a group or by various groups, not an individual. This kind of service needs the participation of human beings who are awakening to higher evolutionary values. These beings may or may not be incarnate.

The most beautiful cases of spiritual communion between higher beings and human beings on the surface of the Earth occur as an outcome of the positive karma generated by some worthy deed carried out jointly in the past, during incarnations in which they were together.

Therefore, acts of cooperation are of value for all eternity and should be practiced and perfected. One way to do this is to be willing to carry out tasks as best possible, whether individually or with others. Evidently, through human perception alone we cannot know what is really the best. But we can desire to know what is best and this, in itself, already produces a deep positive effect.

As soon as we become aware of the law of karma and try to balance out past actions, transformations begin to take place in different ways. Grace and mercy can be drawn down from higher levels of consciousness according to the earnestness of our aspiration. The words of the Bhagavad-Gita[1] spoken by the inner self, assure us that a fundamental and straightforward decision can lead to liberation:

> The one who does My works and has Me as the supreme object, who is devoted to Me and is free from attachment and is without enmity toward all beings, may come to Me.
>
> (XI, 55)

> Works affect Me not, nor have I desire for the fruit of works; he who thus knows Me is not bound by his works.
>
> (IV, 14)

---

[1] *The Gita*, op.cit.

Family Ties in the Karmic Web

Significant karmic ties come into play within a family group. The situations that a soul encounters in the family environment can either help or hinder its growth. Therefore, being able to participate in choosing the family group before incarnating is an important step for the soul. The possibility of taking conscious part in the preparation and formation of its future family environment depends on the soul's level of evolution.

Less evolved souls do not make this choice. They yearn for experiences in the material world so they are attracted to certain couples by emotional and mental links. But to a certain extent souls of average evolution can foresee their family group and even prepare themselves on inner planes to become a part of this group on the physical level.

Souls that are already able to choose their family group do not always decide to live with persons with whom they will have congenial and happy relationships. Since they have already acquired certain maturity, they seek to settle their debts with the world of matter and with their karmic group so that they can become integrated into universal relationships. They plan their incarnation in order to progress on the way to liberation. They know that by doing so they will have to overcome difficulties, especially those created with other beings in the past. Thus, some incarnations are deliberately planned to function as purgation.

However, with or without the possibility of choosing one's family group, the soul about to become incarnate is always placed in the best environment available for its evolution within the law of karma. When the incarnating soul is aware of this, it accepts and understands situations of conflict in the family and is able to cope with them or to turn them into a stimulus for the development of self and of others. Nevertheless, if one does not practice love-wisdom and compassion, the karmic ties go on becoming stronger and tenser and hold one in states of disharmony that bring about even more dismal and frustrating stages.

Karmic bonds between parents and children reflect directly on their process of evolution. If human beings were more receptive to spiritual law they would follow its wise guidance and realize that only a small portion of humanity should bear offspring. However, this is not what happens. Many beings who are still unprepared to incarnate enter the world attracted by the dense magnetism of sexual relationships between those who are not ready to educate or to nurture the growth of others.

Currently the process of incarnation is becoming more disorderly due to widespread sexual promiscuity and a growing number of intentional abortions and unwanted pregnancies. As a result, in most cases the inner rituals of birth on the subtle levels no longer take place.

Formerly births had been organized according to groups of souls which should be together because of their affinity. Nowadays, however, this balanced planning is generally no longer feasible. There are so many opportunities for pregnancy, including by artificial means, that it has become impractical to keep a less evolved soul within its correct cycle of incarnation on the inner levels of existence without intervening in free will. With the doors to the world of matter flung wide open through sexual promiscuity, a soul is naturally drawn to the heavy density of the material world.

In certain cases, to procreate under conditions that are contrary to spiritual progress can slow down the evolution of an incarnating soul, as well as that of the parents, during an entire lifetime. Incarnation then lacks a spiritual basis and it becomes more difficult for the inner energy to vitalize the bodies that will receive the descending soul. Inner energy withdraws even further from the parents. This is the reason for so much lack of understanding and tedium, so much destitution and abandonment, during the years of their family life together.

Many beings could be undergoing healing while they are discarnate. Therefore, couples who prematurely draw unprepared souls down to the physical world, generate a heavy karmic debt. The consequences of this karma could hinder those parents from being able to continue developing satisfactorily.

The time comes when, at some point, the burden of irresponsible procreation, genetic family inheritance and negative karma engendered through hundreds of incarnations, can become too heavy. Personal willpower and aspiration cannot always lighten such a load. In some cases not even the energy of the inner self is able to remove all of the burden, since, in a certain way, the inner being also has to follow the dictates of the law of karma in everything related to the physical levels. Some situations can only be changed with higher, transcendent help.

Although we are living through such chaotic times, never

has higher help been more available. This is because of the profound transformations now being prepared on Earth. Although they are presently being announced, these transformations will fully surface in future times.

Help comes when one really decides to change one's attitudes and no longer lets oneself be carried away by apparently insignificant and fleeting experiences that can cause imbalances for the rest of one's life. Furthermore, help comes when one puts one's faith in supraphysical reality and not just in one's personal abilities. As long as one relies on merely human potential and especially on one's own way of solving problems, one is not truly open to the action of grace. Grace can transform everything.

Based on supra-human laws, grace can remove normally insurmountable obstacles to the ascension of an individual, as well as of a group, of a kingdom of nature or of even wider spheres of life. The consequences of the down-flow of grace are unpredictable: it can heal, transform and raise consciousness to otherwise inaccessible levels. The action of grace can change people and can awaken them to unimaginable realities.

Many current difficulties in family relationship result from the misuse of the human being's creative potential. Today most human energy is channeled into sexual experiences, which are the densest expression of creativity.

However, if one awakens to higher creative activities one begins to become stabilized and one's emotional life is finally subdued. Then it becomes easier for a person to engage in more subtle tasks, in universal works that benefit others. When creative energy is raised, the emotions become strong enough not to get caught up in everyday emotional and mental affairs.

The correct use of creative energy does not imply repression. At a certain point in evolution the personality is more intensely permeated by the soul and inner maturity can be reflected in human relationships. The sexual impulse is quieted and spiritual impulses are more readily embraced.

This transformation is never limited to the individual sphere. It touches other beings who are likewise beginning to enhance and expand their creative expression.

Let us keep in mind some attitudes that help us get along with others within family group relationships without reinforcing karmic ties:

- ✧ to refrain from stirring up conflicts that arise when family members have different interests or choose different paths, which frequently happens in the disorder of the present times;
- ✧ to be as responsible and caring toward family members as toward other persons and to transform and elevate clinging affection and confining attachments that are usually stimulated by customs and traditional culture;
- ✧ to remember, when confronted with an adverse family environment, that one's correct attitudes toward it can be helpful in paying off recent or even far remote karmic debts.

Thus many families function like schools for perfection and opportunities for purgation. When one member acts in an inclusive and spiritual way, which is different from common standards, the other members may become antagonistic. In these cases the person should seek and practice impartiality or neutrality. This will help avoid conflicts. A true fraternal spirit, and not mere emotional and mental involvement, can then emerge and become more and more widely expressed.

Family ties do not necessarily have to be restrictive, but quite often they are. One of the rare, known examples in which family members provided true mutual support was the family of Thérèse of Lisieux.[2] Thérèse's deeply spiritual parents had nine children, of which only five daughters survived. All of them entered the monastic life. The traits of all the family members, without exception, showed that this was a group of souls dedicated more to expressing supra-human energies than to satisfying desires for personal, material and tangible objectives.

Family environments generally lack the quality of energy necessary for them to be fields for the higher evolution of souls. Even well structured families tend to care only about material evolution and to keep up with the norms of society that are frustrating for souls. Souls that have to carry out universal tasks on the physical level need to be in contact with groups that are unrestrained by family ties, groups in which they are given a chance to discover inner relationships and to free themselves from human attachments.

Such opportunities for group life were supposed to have been widely provided on the surface of the Earth. Groups following spiritual goals and a common life of service can express soul groupings that exist on the inner levels, but that are rarely found on the physical level. Therefore, souls having a deep need for teaching have been drawn to inner, supraphysical instruction.

---

[2] Sainte Thérèse de l'Enfant Jésus e de la Sainte Face, *Histoire d'une Âme*, biographical manuscripts [Paris: Edition du Cert, 1972].

At this stage of evolution on the planet, humans are stimulated to become aware of the contacts being made on the supraphysical levels. Important subjective experiences occur while outer human life goes on.

What generally occurs in the inner groups is very different from normal family fellowship. Families tend to stimulate the egocentric aspects of their members, to foster self-fulfillment, to exalt self-centeredness and to impose ties of mutual obligation, especially among parents and children, often in a disguised manner. Because of this, families frequently curb the freedom that their members need in order to follow their destined paths.

Ideally, the family institution should carry out the role of the first teacher, preparing the incarnating beings to discover their own inner guidance and to recognize the part that they are to play in the progress of the world. However, the family is generally incapable of fulfilling this role and incarnating beings find more hindrance than help in their quest for universal realities within the realms of the family's affection and spirituality. Currently, institutions such as the family, religion and the state, which were created to assist inexperienced souls, are disintegrating. Deprived of this backing, one has to rely on an earnest desire to attain spiritual life so as to be able to follow the quest on one's own and with minimal support.

The family, as an institution, carries a heavy karma. This karma is difficult to resolve while family members remain tied to levels of affinity or rejection that cause various problems in their interrelationships. Moreover, for many, the family group as a social unit has lost its meaning.

However, great and radical transformations await us. The present seemingly hopeless situation will be changed. The new form of relationship that is emerging will be based on interaction among souls and no longer on purely human affinity or rejection. In the forthcoming world cycle other significant changes will also occur in the very constitution of the human being.

To solve problems of relationship among people causes widespread repercussions. It even affects planetary development. Presently the Earth receives on its surface many beings who need healing and harmonization and it distils and transforms the impurities that circulate in the solar system. But it will certainly have other functions in the coming ages. Seeds sown today produce tomorrow's fruits, thus making it possible for new and yet unrevealed forms of interrelationship to gradually take shape.

Evolution holds in store forms of existence for humanity of the Earth that are still unknown. It has already been noted that in the future, beings will be born without needing parents. According to the initiate Helena P. Blavatsky,[3] this method of procreation will first be implanted in animals and later on will be extended to the human species. Women will conceive children without the need for fertilization and in distant cycles of the planet individuals will even be able to reproduce themselves on their own.

In a future cycle of humanity, when the composition of the Earth becomes more subtle, the function of the organism will be simplified. Children will not be born from the uterus, the period of gestation will be three months and will not take place within the maternal womb, but in the mother's etheric cosmic center.

---

[3] See Helena P. Blavatsky, *The Secret Doctrine: The Synthesis of Science, Religion and Philosophy*, vol. II — *Anthropogenesis* [London: The Theosophical Publishing Company, Limited, 1888].

In the future, the reproductive organs and certain glands will gradually disappear, as is happening with the ileocaecal appendix today. Some signs of crucial transformation are becoming perceptible to intuitive persons. Indications of the degradation of the human species, such as increasing sterility among young adults, are pointing to profound changes that cannot be accounted for by scientific reasoning alone.

The way in which procreation takes place in a civilization on material levels depends on the evolutionary laws that govern it. In the advanced intraterrestrial and extraterrestrial worlds[4] there is no sexual reproduction because these worlds are composed of matter that is more subtle than that of the surface of the Earth. Sexual reproduction was the means given by nature to terrestrial humanity at a certain stage of its evolution. However, human beings in general have not understood or used this means of reproduction correctly. Even among those who have tried to pattern their lives in keeping with higher precepts, many have misunderstood this process. According to tradition and questionable interpretations, the biblical injunction to "be fruitful and multiply" affirmed that humanity was to reproduce abundantly and this led humans to give way to their desires. However, in a broader sense, this biblical concept implies expansion of consciousness and not the uncontrolled proliferation of the species that has taken place.

A population growth that has been quantitative rather than qualitative is one of the main causes of the chaos on the Earth. Although there are beings who have incarnated with full

---

[4] **Intraterrestrial and extraterrestrial worlds.** Humanity inhabits all of the cosmos in differing states of consciousness and stages of development. Intraterrestrial refers to life on the inner planes of the planet that is not always composed of physical matter. Many extraterrestrial beings are part of the same Humanity-Life of the Races on the Earth's surface, but some belong to very different spheres of existence and even to other galaxies. For further references see: Trigueirinho, *Calling Humanity* [Minas Gerais, Brazil: Irdin Editora, 2002].

awareness of the tasks they were to fulfill for the benefit of the world, these have been very rare. In such cases when a higher task has to be carried out, souls use spiritual will and build a thoughtform[5] strong enough to contact those who will serve as parents on the physical level. Nevertheless, even in these situations they come into physical incarnation by what Sri Aurobindo[6] called the "coarse methods of physical nature."

In the next cycle of the Earth, the continuation of the human species will not depend on sexual drive and intercourse, but on spiritual will and its complementary energies. Although the law of birth will continue to exist for some, humans will be able to enter the material world by means of an interaction on supraphysical levels. The incarnating soul will gather the substance to compose its earthly bodies and the etheric energy of the parents will aid this materialization. Thus the current process of procreation will have been transcended.

---

[5] **Thoughtform.** Conglomeration of energies and forces generated by the power inherent in thought. Its quality varies in accordance with the originating impulse.

[6] **Sri Aurobindo.** (1872 — 1950) His work focused on a yoga that sought to integrate one's inner and outer activities into one life, a manifestation of divine conscious-

Restoring Equilibrium and Healing through Karma

When looked at from a wider perspective, everything has a role in the Plan of Evolution. Within this plan, ailments come about because of the need to bring order into one's life. Ailments are an opportunity for human beings to advance and to balance their negative karma.

Beings who are already conscious on the soul level are aware of their evolutionary goal prior to incarnating. Based on this, they program situations that will provide the necessary developmental experiences during the lifetime about to begin on Earth. Since the soul participates in the design of its own program and has the support of forces made available to it by means of the law of karma, the program always takes into account the level of a person's endurance. In this way, a proposed ailment is never greater than one's capacity to bear it. An ailment only becomes too heavy to bear when the person rejects it or reacts against it.

When an ailment that has been programmed before birth appears, one has to muster up enough strength from within to transcend that state of infirmity. This strength, which would not have been rallied without the ailment, is not to be used to struggle against the infirmity but to face it intelligently and cooperatively, seeing it as an opportunity to bring about equilibrium. For example, someone who had committed theft, either in the present or in a former incarnation, might have to suffer a chronic ailment in the hands. The effort to treat and to adjust patiently to the malady could, in the overall balance of energies, compensate for the past deed.

In order to alleviate pain or bear discomfort, one should resort to the strength that comes from within. Ailments could then bring about new understanding and hence, new habits. In this way, if we learn to grow through personal infirmities we will acquire greater strength that will be used to carry out the development desired by our higher self. In some cases this strengthening can occur and the new potential can emerge during the same incarnation. In other cases we are prepared by means of long-term experiences and the results will only appear in a future life.

There are also cases in which people who tend to take the wrong direction develop infirmities beforehand so they can avoid making choices contrary to what their souls have programmed. For instance, a person who is capable of living in chastity and is destined to do so, yet is unwilling to accept celibacy, could develop either congenital or acquired problems in the genital organs that would limit sexual activity.

According to ancient wisdom, the main function of suffering is to prepare the body to be less susceptible to imbalances. Residues of former dissonant behavior are eliminated from the cells through pain. At the same time other impressions are imprinted on the cells, inducing the person to avoid involvement in similar negative situations.

Much can be balanced out by trials and suffering in the area of health but the beneficial results do not always appear in the same incarnation. In some cases the positive impulse only comes about in a subsequent incarnation. The parts of the body that were purified in the past life are healthy in the new physical body.

Some experiences of illness that one may undergo can be quite revealing. For example, the habit of self-centeredly closing oneself up and not communicating adequately with the outer world and with fellow beings could be balanced out by measles, which sometimes appear even in adulthood. Nevertheless, measles and other diseases are more common during the first years of life so that the person may be released as soon as possible from some basic imbalances stemming from a former life. Vaccination to immunize children against such diseases ignores the reality of the purging effect of certain illnesses. Tendencies considered by the higher self to be undesirable and retrograde could be removed from the new personality. Certain hereditary elements, especially those characteristics that do not serve the purpose of incarnation and that the personality does not want to accept or to which it cannot adapt, could be expelled through fevers.

While fever is burning away undesirable substances present in the physical and subtle bodies, a person receives help to overcome the desire for material and superfluous things and to dissolve physical, emotional and mental illusions. The so-called *realities* of these denser levels of existence are nothing compared to the reality that the higher self is beginning to grasp. Without such means, how could the higher self, confined within an undisciplined personality that is still unaware of broader facts, remove illusions and heal imbalances?

Neuroses, neurasthenia and some cases of hysteria may appear when there is a need to transform a past that has fallen into the deep layers of the subconscious. Nature uses these ailments to dissolve indefinable remnants of what is no longer of use to the being. However, the outcome of some events remains in what is called the 'karmic register', because extensive karmic purification and balancing cannot always be programmed for a single incarnation. So this outcome is compensated for over several lifetimes. However, if with each incarnation on Earth the soul expresses elevated and evolutionary behavior, avoids causing new imbalances, or counteracts its negative past with positive deeds, the karmic purification and balancing does not have to be too long.

Although it is possible to grow in consciousness while discarnate, karmic debts incurred in the physical world normally can only be compensated for in the same world. This is because the material particles have to undergo experiences that are opposite to the previous ones. Thus karmic adjustments are generally carried out during physical life and ailments are effective instruments for bringing about these transformations.

There are several ways to treat ailments of the emotional body. One way, which is no longer valid for those on the spiritual path, is for the person to face up to unresolved nodules from the past, exposing them to psychological analysis. For someone who is able to probe into these things intelligently, such a process could be partially liberating. But rarely is it possible to resolve the obstructions, and it takes years to achieve what inner healing can do almost instantly.

The method of exhaustive psychological reconstruction of events is still frequently used in traditional psychology. However, without transcending the influence of the forces of involution that lie within him or herself, the person cannot undo the karmic knot. The traumatic or disturbing situations will then be repeated, albeit under other guises and using new rationale.

To treat one's emotional body effectively, one should first of all seek inner reconciliation with oneself. This does not imply giving in to forces of involution. Rather, it means accepting one's own shadow side, knowing that this basic and indispensable acceptance is not passive but is the point of departure for a process of transformation focused on the present reality.

From the evolutionary and spiritual standpoint, imperfections stimulate one's progress when they are accepted in order to be transformed. On the other hand, when they are rejected they fail to produce this effect and merely purify the residues of negative actions, feelings and thoughts.

Furthermore, complaining about one's suffering or reacting against it prevents one's character from receiving the moral and spiritual impulses it imparts.

All the inhabitants of this planet have within themselves a vibration that individually identifies them with the cosmic sphere from whence they came to enter the earthly plane. The perception of this vibration may conflict with prevailing mental tendencies. Therefore it is better to abstain from hasty conclusions and from ingrained stereotyped concepts of the conventional mind.

Unless we receive clear indications from supra-mental levels, we know very little about the reasons for what happens in life. However, no matter what might be the underlying reasons, everything that happens in life provides conditions to further our evolution and even our sanctification. Paul Brunton[7] has pointed out that it is our great loss not to feel the need to sanctify our days.

The term 'sanctification' refers to the process of karmic

---

[7] **Paul Brunton.** (1898 — 1981) Philosopher and author who introduced esoteric ideas to the general public of the West. See *The Notebooks of Paul Brunton, Vol. 1, Perspectives* [Burdett, NY: Larson Publications, 1984].

equilibration through the replacement of negative physical actions, feelings and thoughts by positive ones and the subsequent process of making these actions, feelings and thoughts become neutral. Those who have attained a certain degree of mystical fulfillment by being dedicated to this self-purification, manifest virtues, altruism and self-surrender to the spiritual world through faith, devotion and fidelity to the evolutionary laws. 'Sanctification' encompasses different levels of fulfillment. For most people this is still an unexplored area.

All souls are to live this stage of sanctity as they set out to free themselves from attachments, and consequently from karmic bonds. This is not a penitential path. It is a path of progressively letting go of personal human will in order to fulfill a higher inner will that lies within oneself.

In this way, human beings will one day attain true liberation.

Part 3
Liberation from Karma

The Way out of the Labyrinth

Over the ages the law of karma has guided the material evolution of the Earth and will go on guiding it for some time to come. Thus, without meaning to or even knowing it, most human beings have been kept within this law. Karma had to be fulfilled because this was the direction for the evolution of this planet. While this condition still holds true for many, karma is being transcended.

Questions such as, "What have I done to deserve this?" and "When will this come to an end?" have often been raised, implicitly denoting a concept of obligation. However, some people do not ask such questions. For them karma is there and they wisely attempt to bring it into balance without creating stumbling blocks. Thus, they move quickly off the wheel of incarnations.

In these times, more and more people are finding the strength to deal with the effects of their past actions and are on the way to transcending the law of karma. They do so mainly by being dedicated to a supreme and divine power and by facing life situations dispassionately. They are able to put aside the notion that fulfilling an obligation is burdensome. The ones who naturally express the energy of love regard their duties as tasks to be fulfilled because these contribute to the greater good. They do everything with simplicity, without complaining or commenting or engaging in superfluous reasoning — a benign way of moving beyond the sphere of the law of karma.

Another way to transcend the law of karma is through sincere prayer, by being open to higher levels of existence and by surrendering to spiritual goals. However, one should have a clear understanding of what this liberating prayer means.

Prayer, in which one petitions for one's own or another's good, takes place on a human level and inevitably creates karma, even though it might be positive karma. Detached prayer, as a pure offering to the Source of Life, activates supra-mental energies and attracts higher laws.

Surrendering everything to God is said to be the freest and most direct way of praying. If this Supreme Consciousness knows what It does, if It knows us better than we know ourselves, if It ministers to our needs with utmost perfection, how can we ask for anything?

To avoid generating karma in prayer, that is, to refrain from getting caught up in a cycle of debts or retributions, one should focus one's consciousness on the soul level, on the intuitive level, or even higher.

A divine energy, which could be called mercy, raises the human being to levels that are unattainable within the normal processes of the law of karma. This powerful and wise energy flows through impersonal prayer and imparts healing, harmony and liberation.

Despite the fact that, throughout the ages, the word *mercy* has taken on a strong emotional charge, in its purest sense it denotes this energy that heals and transforms on material, human and psychological levels. Through divine mercy, positive karmic residues that remained 'on file' can change situations and bring about circumstances that are more favorable for the development of consciousness.

This mercy is the response given by the inner world to a need felt by individuals, by all humanity or by the planet. For example, divine mercy is manifested when someone has done everything possible to advance along the path to liberation but cannot overcome the limitation of the material bodies. This energy comes from spiritual levels and is the basis for forgiveness. It characterizes the continual help offered to humankind by the Hierarchies,[1] even though humans seldom respond to these incentives.

The principal misunderstanding of those who transgress the law is to consider that their error is greater than divine mercy; because of this, they do not allow themselves to receive it.

Human karma is mainly part of the ego. Therefore, to be able to transcend the sphere of the law of cause and effect, one's soul or a higher nucleus of consciousness must govern one's existence.

Seeking this transcendence with the active participation of the soul that longs for liberation leads to the stages of rising above free will. The gift of free will, in principle, is one of the instruments by which the ego learns and is strengthened. But at more advanced stages of the evolutionary path free will begins to hamper the soul's progress.

---

[1] **Hierarchies.** Consciousnesses that have transcended the material laws and have ascended the sublime steps of spiritual existence. As a unified and cohesive body, they transmit directives for the fulfillment of the evolutionary purpose to the inhabitants of the universe where they work.

Free will is a characteristic that is specific to the human stage of evolution on Earth. It is the ability to make one's own choice regarding the action to be carried out. Up to this time free will has generally been based on tendencies that are personal and often obscure. The exercise of free will determined many of the present features of the planet and, among others, the state of physical and psychological contamination into which it has plummeted.

Over the ages a few human beings have managed to overcome free will, to expand their consciousness and to rise above the level of the majority. These beings have opened the way for others and currently more and more humans are advancing in this way. Free will is a part of human cosmogony linked to the chakra energy system, which is now being replaced.

When one masters free will by seeking to accomplish the transpersonal will within oneself, a new energy begins to permeate one's consciousness, bringing a greater evolutionary impulse and granting a broad view of the purpose of one's individual or group life, or of planetary life. Human beings advance toward free will in stages.

- As primitive beings, humans do not, in fact, make any choices. They are governed by the impulses of the forces that move in their bodies. Their destinies are traced strictly within the law of karma. They hardly ever participate in determining their destiny.

- In human beings of average evolution, the forces of desire and thought struggle for supremacy over actions. This is when free will reaches its highest expression. This confrontation lasts until the forces of thought prevail and, at a more advanced stage, become united to the will of the inner self.

❖ When the soul begins to guide the personality, although, free will is still present, it ceases to prevail. Really relevant events, whether for one's own evolution or for a service to be rendered, are determined by one's deeper inner cores and by the Hierarchies who inspire them.

❖ Finally, when a soul takes over the total guidance of the personality, free will is transcended.

In this way, higher laws gradually begin to rule human existence, replacing the law of karma. The transformation that is currently taking place in an increasing number of beings is directing them toward the essence of spiritual and divine life. Surrendering to this essence leads them to overcome free will and to dissolve the boundaries of the ego that keep material consciousness separated from its inner source.

Liberation by Fulfilling Broader Laws

When human beings enter the world of matter they bring the key of their cosmic origin concealed within themselves. The history of humanity has been, and continues to be, painful because this inner key has remained forgotten even though it has always been accessible.

Unrestricted and unconditional faith in the existence of a supreme intelligence above all things, is one of the means to discover this key, for it opens the way to awareness of immortality. This kind of faith holds subtle energies that lead a person to live a life in accordance with laws that are above the material ones.

Karma is gradually transformed when one changes one's attitudes. However, the real transformation of karma is based on this faith and on the support of the Hierarchies who inspire humans to fulfill cosmic designs in outer life. As this transformation takes place, one is increasingly liberated from compulsory physical, emotional and mental ties and can enter incarnation with clearly defined purposes, such as to serve the Plan of Evolution.

As we grow in consciousness our understanding of the law of karma changes. We cease considering the law of karma merely as an instrument to compensate for past errors and begin to recognize it as an infallible and extremely useful means to fulfill the higher goal of life. We begin to discover this goal when we intensify our detachment. We begin to perceive that the law of karma is present on various levels of life and that it operates in different ways. We then start to cooperate with karma in an intelligent manner and do not resist the transformation proposed by the higher will. No longer just performers of our destiny, we become effective participants of evolution, true co-creators.

Therefore our material and psychic constitution can be entirely changed if we base ourselves on faith. We can gradually rediscover the key that opens the portals to our immortal reality, a reality where there is no yesterday or tomorrow, only an eternal now without any karma. Faith is a beacon that illuminates our journey through the murky byways of the material worlds and leads us steadily toward higher laws.

Many souls who have undertaken the clearing up of their karma during several incarnations can now have their personalities ruled by higher laws. However, they remain subject to the law of karma because of human inertia or lack of daring to take on a new state.

In general, these beings have matured through experience and are not swayed by the common misdeeds of the majority. However, they hold on to some behaviors that are traditionally considered positive but which hinder their leap into the unknown. Personal responsibilities are so important for them that they relegate spiritual and universal works to secondary importance.

Those who delay in letting go of what is no longer meant for them are sometimes catapulted out of their lethargy by the loss of possessions or by a disharmonious severing of emotional ties. Such losses can cause the personality to suffer, but for the inner self, which pursues deeper and freer development, they are long-awaited opportunities.

The impulses sent from above to bring about these ruptures never come prematurely. They wait for the personality to have acquired sufficient strength to take on the newly unfolding phase with the minimum possibility of falling back. When people go beyond a routine way of life, where everything already seems familiar, they experience a fullness that only the absence of personal ties can grant.

It takes an iron will to dissolve the ties that bind consciousness to ego, with its habits and vices, and to go beyond what is possible for the majority. This can be done by renouncing one's ideas, opinions and preferences and by stripping oneself of all that is superfluous. This is the only way to reach the higher laws, where karma does not exist.

The New Testament states that those called to follow the Master were exhorted not to waste time looking back for they were to announce the Kingdom of God. Today, those who are able to exercise their will power in this way experience an indescribable lightness. No longer hampered by the web of karma, they announce this kingdom through works of a transcendent nature.

As we free ourselves we learn that nothing is lost when we renounce something or someone. Once we detach ourselves, we can find again what was put aside in an inconceivably more elevated and essential way. We discover that we are united to an all-embracing Consciousness. Our attachment to our memories of habitual relationships and of the past can hinder our perception of this real unity. If we do not put aside these attitudes, they can keep on intruding.

Expansion of consciousness, as well as commitment to higher goals, reduces the influence of the law of karma. Nonetheless, from a more precise point of view, karma only ceases to operate when one's consciousness is really united to the Source of Life. In this state of Oneness there is no longer a separation between giver and receiver, no difference between Creator and creature. This deeply inward condition, impossible to describe in words, is only revealed to those who have the courage to rise above the trivial way of life lived by the majority.

Part 4

Beyond Karma

Monadic Transmutation

We are beginning to be aware of changes in the system of birth and death on Earth and of a law beyond the sphere of karma — the law of monadic transmutation. Although this law has been operative on this planet for a long time, only now is it being more widely disclosed. In past eras very few knew about monadic transmutation and only in rare, special cases did this law govern entrance into the world of matter.

As the law of monadic transmutation is applied to this earthly humanity, it completely changes the way an inner self enters the material world. A new freedom follows the manifestation of this law. It transcends the unending turning of the wheel of incarnations under the law of karma.

The monad is our nucleus that is deeper than the soul. It is also called spirit or cosmic essence and is revealed when our consciousness expands. The monadic will is higher than the will of a soul. This is why, in some Christian writings, the monad is referred to as the Father. In monadic transmutation the monad withdraws from the personality and gives it up to another, more evolved monad. The outgoing monad will have completed the evolutionary stage planned for that incarnation. The incoming monad transmutes in order to carry out a task on the material levels and is not under the law of incarnation. Thus both monads grow in light and consciousness.

Monadic transmutation is governed by higher laws. The law of karma is no longer applied to both monads in this stage of evolution. In the way transmutations are occurring in these times, the incoming monad takes on the karma of the mental, emotional and physical-etheric bodies it enters but maintains a certain control over them. This monad is free from karma, but the same cannot be said for the bodies, because they carry hereditary influences and the past history of their atoms on this planet.

In monadic transmutation the outgoing monad transcends the law of death and it will no longer incarnate under the law of karma. Through this process the incoming monad now transcends the law of physical birth, if it had not already been transcended.

The incoming monad is spared the need to go through stages of uterine gestation, infancy and adolescence. These are all unnecessary for the task to be fulfilled. By entering bodies that are able to perform the designated task, this monad remains in incarnation only during the time needed to carry out its task. So this transmuted being is exempt from the law of karma as well as from the law of reincarnation.

Many extraterrestrial beings enter through monadic transmutation when they need to serve on the physical level on Earth. Monadic transmutation will also become accessible to the majority of inhabitants of the surface of the Earth in their forthcoming evolutionary stage.

Under the law of monadic transmutation human beings cross over to the supraphysical world freed from attachments to what they are leaving behind here on Earth, and released from anxiety about what they will find on the inner side of life. Those who come into physical life are spared the traumas caused by gestation and birth and by the stages of growth and formation, in preparation for life on Earth.

※

Various spiritual instructors have alluded to monadic transmutation. Rudolf Steiner (1861 — 1925) affirmed that at a certain point in evolution, an individual could need conditions that are different from those initially provided. When reaching a certain age, a human being could suddenly go through a near-death experience or fall into an outright faint during which a transformation could occur, with the Inner Self leaving the body and another Inner Self taking it over. Steiner says that this kind of exchange of Inner Selves could happen in diverse situations and the phenomenon is known by all occultists.[1]

In 1920, the Tibetan Master Djwal Khul, whose teachings were transmitted to the West by Alice A. Bailey (1880 — 1949), referred to this phenomenon as a 'divine obsession', and assured us that it would be increasingly common in the years to come. Through this 'divine obsession' an individual would cooperate willingly with the One who would inspire, take over or use his or her lower vehicles (mental, emotional and physical-etheric). This is always done in order to render greater service to humanity. This process of exchange will become more frequent and better understood when the human race develops continuity of consciousness between the physical and emotional bodies and later on, between these and the mental body.[2]

Monadic transmutation is carried out under the benevolent

---

[1] See Rudolf Steiner, *Das Lukas Evangelium* (The Gospel of St. Luke) 8th Edition [Dornach, Switzerland: Verlag Gesamtausgabe, 1985], p. 114.

[2] See Alice A. Bailey, *Letters on Occult Meditation* [New York: Lucis Publishing Company, 1950].

aura of liberated beings and their energy sustains the entire process. Evolved devas[3] also take part. The outgoing monad is released from its karma and a vibratory channel is created to permit the entrance of the new monadic energy. These processes would not be possible without the participation of energies that are higher than the monadic ones.

Concepts such as monadic transmutation are still unknown to most people. In this regard, one could recall Goethe's statement that man cannot arrive at the understanding of anything unless he loves it. The great poet was referring to the need to grasp subtle facts through the feelings of the heart rather than through the reasoning of the mind.

---

[3] **Devas.** A Sanskrit word meaning "beings of light" that includes those we call angels. They build all existing forms.

The New Genetic Code

The genetic code of a human being is much more than a physical-chemical configuration; it is a set of conditions of energy determined by the archetype for humanity in each evolutionary cycle. It is not limited to the configuration of the substances of an organism, nor to its functioning, but it includes its state of consciousness. The genetic code goes beyond the level of matter, and is an instrument for the Plan of Evolution to guide human beings toward the energy pattern they are destined to express.

Since it is a means to bring about the materialization of archetypal patterns and since these patterns are dynamic, whenever necessary a genetic code is modified or substituted by those who govern evolution. Such adjustments are made when human beings move beyond the archetypal pattern of a given cycle, or when there is a change in the cycle. In the history of this humanity there have been at least four shifts in the genetic code.

Humanity has reached an impasse in failing to go beyond polarization on the most concrete levels of life. This impasse has been added to what is happening on the Earth, a planet that is to become subtle and to be transferred to an etheric level, free of the present density. This situation calls for profound transformations. Consequently, a more powerful nonmaterial impulse was needed.

Thus, a new genetic code, GNA,[4] is beginning to be implanted on supraphysical levels of humanity.

This planet is becoming progressively more subtle. Therefore, the humanity that will inhabit it will have to have adequate genetic components to be able to express what the planetary consciousness requires as it ascends.

The new genetic code is being introduced into approximately ten percent of the human beings, incarnate or not, within the Earth's environs. On the physical plane the bodies will become more subtle; on the spiritual plane this will happen according to the specific laws of that plane.

Until now, hereditary traits, such as height, skin color, physical features, presence or absence of physical defects, as well as some psychological tendencies, have been passed on from parents to offspring through chromosomes. This is precisely what is beginning to change.

For those who are receiving GNA, all this old structure of heredity and karma falls away. GNA is of a stellar and nonmaterial origin. Therefore, under this new genetic code, individuals are not conditioned by the past experiences of their species.

DNA, the genetic code activated in the cycle currently coming to a close, is of animal origin and could only take humanity up to a certain level of evolution. The new genetic code, GNA, is now needed in order to open the way for a greater integration into inner realities.

---

[4] **GNA.** This acronym does not denote a specific chemical substance, but an electromagnetic field.

When human beings still have DNA and are governed by the law of karma, their actions on the physical plane create material values and generate either abundance or scarcity, according to the quality of their deeds. Through their feelings humans create values on the level of pleasure and dissatisfaction, thus engendering positive or negative emotional situations, according to the nature of these values. Through their thoughts they create values on the level of ideas, which produce either high ideals and consequent mental health, or pessimism, criticism and disharmony, depending on the quality of their thoughts.

With the new genetic code, human beings will no longer be held captive by their own limited creations. Furthermore, they will lose all aggressiveness and will be able to understand that all goods belong to everyone and not only to a few, and that these goods should be applied in developing spiritual consciousness and not in satisfying egoism.

Because of its origin, GNA gives human beings stability, unity of thought and a sense of fraternity, thus making it possible for them to live consciously on inner levels and within the laws that govern them. A new vibration is introduced into their subjective world with the implanting of this new genetic code. This vibration is projected from level to level, drawing all the atoms of their bodies into attunement with its frequency, which is subtle and is in accordance with the cosmic goal of their higher self.

In everyday life we should do that which is good, beneficial and useful, detached from any and all fruits of our action, so that we can prepare for the transition from the law of karma to the higher law of evolution. This teaching is as ancient as the world.

But only now, with the implanting of the new genetic code, can the teaching be understood and carried out by a greater number of people. Under the old DNA code even those who seek a spiritual life behave like the Apostle Paul, who declared in one of his epistles that he did not do the good he wanted to do, but did the evil he did not want to do.

However, the forthcoming expansion of consciousness is not based solely on changing the genetic code, or on transcending the law of karma. Up until now, only the cells of coarser vibration have been active, especially in the brain, and these cells have had to endure the disorder of human bodies. Nevertheless, a large contingent of cells, destined to pick up and manifest energy waves coming from the spiritual and divine planes, will be awakened.

The awakening of these cells is part of a broad restructuring of this humanity's physical life and depends on the contact that material consciousness has with the soul. This inner contact will bring about a perception that is increasingly freed from egoism and that is less inclined to be linked to people, things and circumstances. In a not too distant future, many people who have a larger portion of active healthy cells will be capable of embracing what is apparently unpleasant in order to help the evolution of groups and of the planet. They will transcend the plane of desire and be able to freely serve the constructor-energies that are performing evolutionary works in the cosmos.

The new genetic code, GNA, can also be developed and manifested on the denser planes of existence, whenever people are receptive to what it inspires and stimulates. Those who are not open to transformation may reject the new code, which then withdraws to subjective levels until the nodules of resistance are dissolved. Depending on the degree of reaction contrary to the nonmaterial impulses prompted by GNA, this genetic code may even be canceled and the person may only become integrated into this evolutionary current in a future cycle.

When the new genetic code becomes fully implanted and abided by, human beings will tend to express unity of aspirations and goals on their mental level. GNA draws cosmic patterns of life down to the Earth and builds the foundations for the New Humanity. It predisposes human beings to become more subtle and its vibration opens the doors of consciousness to experiences and to life on higher planes. Through GNA the energy potential of these planes causes matter to become more fluid. This process, in close collaboration with the soul, has the role of furthering and heightening maturity of consciousness.

The capacity to receive GNA is determined by one's inner affinity with what is radiated by the code itself. GNA should correspond to the aspirations of those who receive it; thus individuals both attract it, and are attracted by it. The subtle action that this genetic code can carry out to fashion life according to the pulsation of the spirit is still a mystery to most people. It will continue to be a mystery until purity and surrender to the higher law, the law of love-wisdom, has become the blueprint for human progress.

Once they have completed their earthly karma, the new human beings will have other resources available to them because their bodies will be purer, more sublime and divested of free will. With the new genetic code implanted in them, human beings will have greater access to knowledge and will fulfill the tasks specified by the new law of evolution. They will express true love and will know that they are part of a harmony that integrates them, once and for all, into the order of the more advanced universes.

By aspiring to ascend to higher levels, without causing harm or transgressing the law of love, human beings will develop undisclosed potentialities. By obeying this sublime law, their own ascent will be assured and this will reflect on all humanity. They will live in unity more freely. Their lives will flow in the steadfast harmony of the spiritual levels of the cosmos that will finally be manifested here on Earth.

Awakening of the Right Side Consciousness

Human beings go through life building links to things, ideas, people, tendencies and forms of life. These links are registered in a part of human consciousness called the left side consciousness. The power of karma, as well as the inclination toward desire and other factors that have drawn this civilization into decadence, are also located in the left side consciousness.

Nevertheless, there is another part of human consciousness that is capable of bringing equilibrium to the tendencies of the left side consciousness and of establishing harmony with the higher laws. This is the right side consciousness, which creates linkages with the abstract levels where archetypal patterns and directives for the Plan of Evolution are revealed. The left side consciousness, in turn, pertains to acquiring knowledge through the external senses and to reproducing familiar patterns. Therefore, it infers association with concrete facts, trivial ideas and ordinary ways of living, perpetuated by customs and all kinds of traditions.

Certain concepts regarding the etheric level of existence are important in order to understand the changes that will permit some humans to transcend the law of karma.

Electric circuits running through the etheric body convey the nerve impulses that reveal to the physical organs the kind of conduct needed to keep the whole organism functioning well. The etheric body also provides the force of cohesiveness for the physical body.

While agglomerations of cells form the organs of the physical body, which, in turn, comprise systems, the etheric body is made up of interconnected nuclei of energies. The level of one's physical health and harmony depends on the degree of clearness of these energy circuits.

There is a countless number of energy circuits in the etheric body, although not all are of equal importance. Some are pivotal while others rotate around them. The paths traced by energy in these circuits, as well as the nuclei activated in them, correspond to the human being's need for expression and for relationship with the surrounding universe.

These circuits are manifested according to each person's level of sensitivity and of spiritual maturity. In this way, the etheric body of someone who focuses on dense things is different from the etheric body of someone whose life is grounded in altruism. The energy centers in action in one body are different from those acting in another. But despite these individual aspects, there is one model for the etheric body of all the members of the human family during a given evolutionary cycle.

There are seven centers or vortices of energy located in the aura close to the spinal column in the etheric body of a human being who still has DNA genetic code and who is governed by the law of karma. These centers are called chakras.

Instructors of the past drew attention to these chakras and used them as a basis to present keys for conscious evolutionary work. For example, *A Treatise on White Magic*[5] points out that living a pure and upright life is the simplest form of adjusting the energies to evolutionary needs and of awakening dormant vital mechanisms and structures.

```
              Head center
              Ajna center
              Throat center
              Heart center
         Solar plexus center
              Sacral center
         Base of spine center
```

The seven chakras related to DNA genetic code

According to this teaching and to many others based on the system of chakras, the personality, which is the material aspect of the human being, reaches its peak when the latent energies at the base of the spine rise to the head and are carried to the center between the eyes, the ajna center. Later, when the energies from the sacral center are sublimated, reoriented and elevated to the throat center, and when the sexual drive has been transcended, the person becomes a conscious creator-force in the higher worlds. Furthermore, when the energies of the solar plexus become transmuted and reoriented to the heart center, the human being will attain group consciousness and become a server of humanity.

This was the work of energy elevation developed throughout the cycle presently coming to a close. However, nowadays

---

[5] See Alice A. Bailey, *A Treatise on White Magic* [New York: Lucis Publishing Company, 1951].

this chakra circuit is being discontinued and a new circuit, that of the right side consciousness, is beginning to be activated in some pioneering individuals. The energy gradually shifts from one system to the other. To understand this process one must bear in mind that:

- ✧ Each stage of planetary development has a basic etheric structure, an archetypal pattern to be manifested;
- ✧ A new planetary and solar cycle began on 8/8/88 (August 8, 1988), with a period of intense purification on Earth and thus the levels of consciousness on the planet are undergoing profound transformations;
- ✧ A new genetic code will govern the formation of the bodies of today's human beings.

In this way, the energy potential available to humans is increasing, and the energy source which was formerly distributed through seven main centers (the chakras) is now concentrated in three centers — the right side mental center, the heart center and the cosmic center.

First supraluminary center
Second supraluminary center
Right side mental center
Right side heart center
Right side cosmic center

The centers of the right side consciousness
related to the new genetic code

Later this potential will expand and two more centers, called supraluminaries, will be added to the three centers that have already become activated. If we look closely, we will see that this *new* energy system in humanity was already implicit in ancient teachings and, in an esoteric way, in the more advanced concepts of the sayings of spiritual sages, such as Sri Aurobindo. However, it was only with the transition that occurred on 8/8/88 (August 8, 1988), that these concepts were finally disclosed.

In the shift from the chakra system to the right side consciousness system, the energy from the head center, the ajna center and part of the throat center merges into a single center, the right side mental center. This is where the cognitive and creative capacities will be unified, bringing human beings greater equilibrium in their interaction with the outer world. Analytical and concrete mental activity will gradually move to the sub-conscious sphere and become automatic, similar to the organic functions of the physical body today.

The heart center synthesizes the energy of the heart center of the former system of chakras and receives part of the energy of the solar plexus and of the throat center. The potential for impersonal love and for creativity will thus be united and will function together. This will totally change relationships among human beings. Difficulties stemming from self-centered interactions will no longer exist, for the heart center is more open to the vibration of the soul, the nucleus in which fraternal life is a reality.

The energies channeled through the sacral and the base of the spine centers, as well as those channeled through the solar plexus, converge at the center located on the right side of the body, below the last rib, the cosmic center. Therefore, the sublimation of the instinctive aspects carried out by evolutionary work based on the system of chakras is being superseded. Individuals whose right side consciousness centers are activated will no longer have their energy focused on such a dense level and the raising of this energy will mean a much greater expansion of consciousness.

Centers of the right side consciousness	Chakras that are being absorbed into the centers of the right side consciousness
Right side mental center	Head center
	Ajna center
	Throat center
Right side heart center	Throat center
	Heart center
	Solar plexus center
Right side cosmic center	Solar plexus center
	Sacral center
	Base of spine center

The relationship of the right side consciousness centers to the chakras

The raising of the energy in these centers of a human being is a natural outcome of the shift in polarization of consciousness. Therefore, nothing should be done to induce it. On the outer levels, the complete transfer from the former chakra system to the right side consciousness circuitry comes about through a spontaneous uplifting of energy, from the quelling of the ego and from the renunciation of free will. In this way, the forces of the ego become integrated into the energies of the soul, which makes it easier for individuals to acquire more self-control and to contact supraphysical laws, especially the higher law of evolution.

This brief account can give one an idea of the effect these transformations have upon transcending the law of karma. Everything that ties human beings to the chain of actions and reactions becomes permeated and governed by other, more subtle, laws. The quality of vibration, which the vortices of the right side consciousness bring about, enables a person to attune to frequencies that are above the ordinary ones of today.

Transition from the left side consciousness to the right side consciousness is not abrupt, for it accompanies an entire reorganization of the energy structure of the bodies of the personality (mental, emotional and physical-etheric). Gradually a new way of looking at facts begins to emerge, replacing the former, more restricted and selfish way. One immediate outcome is that the awakening of the right side consciousness links a human being to laws that are more subtle than the law of karma, especially the higher law of evolution. The person enters a current into which the harmony in the universes can merge without impediment. Right side consciousness is based on communion and brings out the peaceful nature in beings, thus making it possible to vibrate on supraphysical and cosmic levels.

Part 5

Karma in the Life of the Planets

Ties That Go beyond the Ages

In the same way that human beings, in their profound and nonmaterial essence, are spirits or monads, a celestial body is a logos, a nucleus of consciousness and pure energy. Each logos develops and has reached a specific evolutionary stage. This accounts for the differences among celestial bodies.

The logos of the Earth governs its evolution according to its highest purpose of existence and it encompasses everything that is present in its sphere. However, despite this guidance and the intense work of the spiritual Hierarchies in charge of fulfilling this purpose, outer life of the Earth has reached an acute level of conflict because of humanity's misuse of free will.

A planet is more than a mere celestial body; it is a universe composed of several worlds, levels and dimensions. It gradually comes into being through the convergence of currents of life that have their origin in diverse points of the cosmos, especially in the solar system to which it belongs.

The conflicts that are taking place now on Earth stem from various causes, such as:

✧ karmic debts engendered by the planet and by the solar system, which have to be offset;

✧ the heterogeneous way the Earth was inhabited in the

present evolutionary cycle. Beings who transmigrated to the Earth came from different areas of the universe and not all of them had positive experiences before becoming human. So they brought unresolved antagonisms and deep traumas with them;

✧ the fact that the human races which have been living together on the Earth still have karmic accounts to settle, as can be seen by their behavior. Acute differences remain unresolved and these give rise to the numerous wars and chronic hostilities.

As it experienced its stages of evolution, humanity continued reinforcing its choice of free will. As it lost contact with states of purity, its karma tended to become progressively heavier. Nevertheless, these deviations always occurred within the limits permitted by higher laws that prevail over the realities governed by lower laws.

One of the outcomes of this intensification of human karma on Earth, which is an non-sacred planet,[1] was the appearance of diseases intended to bring about collective purging. The first one, syphilis, arose in ancient Lemuria[2] as the consequence of sexual promiscuity among primitive humans, and between humans and animals.

Tuberculosis was another planetary disease. It came up in Atlantis[3] as an element to restore balance. At that time humanity

---

[1] **Non-sacred planet.** A planet which has not yet fully incorporated the aspects and attributes of the logoic solar consciousness, therefore it radiates conflictive energy on denser levels of vibration.

[2] **Lemuria.** A continent that has disappeared. A large part of it is located on the bed of what is now the Pacific Ocean. During the Lemurian age human beings developed their physical body.

[3] **Atlantis.** A continent that has disappeared. Most of it lies on the bed of the present Atlantic Ocean. During the Atlantean age, which followed the Lemurian Age, human beings developed their emotional body.

quelled much of the spiritual progress it could have attained by failing to develop all the inner human resources available to it.

This self-imposed limitation continues until today and is evident in the difficulty individuals find in letting go of familiar levels of consciousness to enter into new planes.

Cancer, a planetary disease, has come to purify human beings and to neutralize their ancient wrongdoing. As science keeps these planetary diseases in check and they cease to be fatal, new ones appear, such as AIDS, while many other diseases are still undetected.

Certain epidemic diseases act as instruments of judgment[4] causing many people to disincarnate. Epidemics are one of the means used by nature to restore the order that was lost on the planet due to overpopulation. Many of those who disincarnate through such diseases enter the subtle levels in a kind of prolonged deep sleep until the door of a new planetary situation is opened to them. However, this is not the general rule.

The Earth is paying off its grossest karmic debts by means of epidemics and other forms of selection. This becomes a way for the Earth to prepare for new cycles governed by a higher, nonmaterial evolution.

At first glance one might be led to think that the spiritual Hierarchies could give greater assistance to the long-suffering humanity of the surface of the Earth. However, one must bear in mind the dependency that humans have developed on the law of karma. As humanity rises above this sphere it will be able to receive greater gifts. These gifts have always been awaiting it. For example, one could recall the New Testament accounts of Mary

---

[4] **Judgment.** A process of selection whereby the vibrations of a specific sphere become homogeneous and attune to a new evolutionary cycle. Logoic consciousnesses and elevated entities carry out judgment seeking the higher good of all.

Magdalene and of Paul of Tarsus, the life of Saint Augustine and many others, who broke out of fairly dense vibratory conditions and in the same incarnation reached levels of communion with cosmic realities and with members of these Hierarchies.

In its present phase the Earth is receiving strong impulses for human beings to seek these gifts. This will only happen more fully when the dissonant deeds of these last eras have been balanced. The forces of nature, also guided by elevated consciousnesses, will intervene in a powerful way to bring about this balance. Each individual will receive the exact measure of return for transgressions committed, because the law of karma is precise and just.

With this global purification the Earth will change its vibratory level and it will be able to follow other laws that shape the ascending evolution of the planets. From then on the Earth will be among the planets that consciously share, preserve and deepen cosmic fraternity.

The Karma of the Evolving Kingdoms on Earth

Not only humankind, but also the creatures of all the kingdoms of nature and all the particles of the tangible world, have karmic debits and credits.

While human beings have individual karma, the situation is different for the subhuman kingdoms. Except for the animals closer to individualization[5] that reincarnate and begin to build their souls, the evolution of animals, plants and minerals is based on the karma of the species to which they belong, as well as the karma of the matter that makes up their physical bodies.

According to the law of karma, each being of the subhuman kingdoms receives a part of the retribution for the interaction that the whole species carries out with the universe. Furthermore, for each animal, plant or mineral species there is a regent-entity that acts as transformer of the energies flowing between the group soul[6] and the beings of the respective species. Extremely elevated

---

[5] **Individualization.** The formation of the individualized soul which takes place through the transition of a monad from the animal kingdom to the human kingdom.

[6] **Group soul.** Nucleus through which the essence of the beings that evolve in the mineral, plant and animal kingdoms is expressed and enters into contact with physi-cal levels. A group soul receives the experiences of each being in that group, synthe-sizes them and shares these experiences with all the others.

solar consciousnesses, which coordinate the application of the law of karma on the level of the solar system, work with this regent-entity.

In the human kingdom each individual receives retribution for his or her deeds and a part of the requital for the deeds of humanity as a whole. This process is different in the subhuman kingdoms for in their case each being is 'the whole species.'

The role of humanity is of utmost importance because the subhuman kingdoms seek to become the human kingdom, a goal they will attain someday, somewhere in the cosmos. Humankind acts as the intermediary between the beings of those kingdoms and the emanations of the spiritual kingdom. However, humans are usually inclined toward tendencies of involution. Because of this they direct the life currents of these kingdoms toward questionable aims and, in doing so, they aggravate their own karma.

Humankind builds a heavy karmic debt by being directly or indirectly involved in polluting the soil, water and air, in devastating forests and in slaughtering millions of animals. Even persons with lofty aspirations have actually contributed to this state of things. However, those who choose to balance these debts will be able to do so in good time.

Energy flows with special intensity over those who have decided to change the conditions that keep them imprisoned. The consequences of unbalanced actions committed in the past can be offset by carrying out opposite actions. Even though the deeds might have been serious, one must keep in mind that divine mercy never fails. The well-known law states, "The last shall be first."

According to esoteric science, negative and dense thoughts and words are greatly responsible for the destructive occurrences in nature and for the savagery of subhuman creatures. The aggressiveness emanated by humans, their hateful and destructive thoughts and their cruel slaughter of animals have a negative repercussion on the inner nuclei of the species. Although for the animal kingdom this is partly a repayment of karmic debts owed the human kingdom, its consequences are serious. These debts were incurred during bygone ages when gigantic animals decimated primitive humanity, not only on the physical, but also on the etheric and astral levels.

However, some human beings are slowly becoming aware of the help that should be given to the animal kingdom. Today many animals are preparing to enter the human kingdom in a future cycle, so they are beginning to form individual souls. These souls develop favorably in nonviolent conditions and protected from contact with the dense vibrations of an environment of sexual promiscuity among humans.

Animals that are preparing for their individualization require differential treatment. Their relationship with human beings must be fraternal, so as to become imbued with the state of consciousness that will be their next evolutionary level. Their development is greatly enhanced in environments where instinctive forces are not commonplace, where there is order and where life is guided by unconditional love. Such environments make it easier for the animal to shift its focus from the sacral area to the heart and mental areas. The nuclei of these higher areas will serve as a basis for the evolving soul to mature serenely.

The plant kingdom has been able to fulfill its purpose for existence on Earth in a special way; consequently, it can contribute greatly to the karmic balancing that the planet is currently undergoing. This kingdom has a meaningful role in the transmutation of etheric vibrations. It has not attained even higher fulfillment because of the density of the psychic field of the present civilization. However, the plant kingdom is not free of negative karma, as one can perceive from the destruction it has suffered all over the world.

With the purification and judgment underway throughout the planet, some species that do not correspond to the future vibration to be instated in the plant kingdom will cease to exist. Others, having completed their cycles of service, will also disappear. After this karmic balance and the renewal of species, communication between humans and plants will be deepened. Agriculture, which at present is targeted solely toward providing for human sustenance, will be replaced with collaboration that is reciprocal and creative.

Because it has fulfilled its part in the current phase of the Plan of Evolution for the Earth, the plant kingdom has opened a way to higher levels of existence, a path that will be followed by the other kingdoms in the future.

As it evolves, the mineral kingdom develops the ability to be selective. It does this when it expresses the wide range of its specimens and provides unique characteristics for each one through the precise interaction of atoms and molecules.

The karmic situation of the mineral kingdom is the same as that of matter itself. The mineral kingdom carries considerable karmic debts. These can be seen in the contamination of the environment caused by human beings, as well as in the transformation wrought by the forces of nature on the crust of the Earth. After the complete purification of the Earth, new forms will be molded in this kingdom and it will have a deeper interaction with the other kingdoms.

Minerals are currently undergoing an intense process of becoming more subtle and in the future cycle they will be recognized as focal points for extra-planetary energies. Once it reaches a more balanced stage, humanity will no longer use crystals, stones and metals in a distorted manner and will be able to work and cooperate with the mineral kingdom in an evolutionary way.

A large part of the chemical elements that make up minerals and the bodies present on this planet have radioactive nuclides in a proportion that is carefully controlled by the Intelligences that govern nature. These radioactive elements are the result of the condensation of cosmic forces introduced into matter and not assimilated by it. They are transformed in cyclic processes in which the excess cosmic forces are absorbed into matter, until they reach the non-radioactive stage

Causing an imbalance in the proportion of radioactive to non-radioactive particles interferes in the ability of the material substratum of the planet to receive and process sidereal forces. For this reason, humans cause a change in the Earth's interaction with extra-planetary life when they manipulate atomic energy.

Paul Brunton[7] has pointed out that scientists have actually destroyed the atom, the prime matter created and used by God to form the universe. Brunton explains that releasing destructive forces and casting them into the world has brought degenerating

---

[7] See *The Notebooks of Paul Brunton, V. 7, Part 2. Healing of the Self / The Negatives* [Burdett, NY, USA: Larson Publications, 1986].

forces into the midst of humanity. He alerts us to the fact that even peaceful commercial use of nuclear energy in reactors is potentially devastating and security measures are unable to avert this threat.

Because of the current density of the Earth, most people understand very little about the elemental kingdom and have only very general notions about the forces that make up this kingdom. When stimulated to carry out tasks, these forces can take on the form of beings, some of which are called the elementals of the earth, water, fire and air. In the future, humanity will have a deeper knowledge of these elementals.

We know today that since these elemental forces are intrinsic to the different levels of consciousness, the elemental kingdom is not following the Plan of Evolution closely and each time it moves away from the goals of the plan, it incurs karmic debt.

The elemental kingdom is at the base of the Earth's evolutionary chain and works together with the other kingdoms. Its karmic balance is almost always brought about by the violent action of the etheric energies coming from both the cosmos and the center of the Earth to adjust the vibratory pattern of the earthly substance to the pattern determined by the planetary regent. The use of nuclear technology and weapons by human beings deters the elemental kingdom's karmic balance.

The kingdom of the devas, including the angelic beings, responds perfectly to the designs of the planetary and cosmic

Hierarchies and therefore this kingdom does not generate karma. The functional structure of the devic kingdom is also stratified. Each devic echelon is in charge of specific and complementary tasks, such as: to receive and transmit archetypal ideas, to build etheric molds for the materialization of these ideas, to constantly adjust created patterns to the original norm and to destroy obsolete patterns.

Devas and angels inhabit supraphysical planes. They evolve by carrying out the purpose that they are given to know, and not by acquiring experience in any temporal succession of events. They do not seek results in their work because they are not involved in what they do. Their field of consciousness is free from bonds, attachments and distortions, which helps them remain outside of the sphere of the law of karma. Therefore this kingdom is a vital point of reference for human beings.

Humanity's conscious relationship with the kingdom of devas is essential for the fulfillment of the Plan of Evolution but it requires utmost purity. This relationship will be developed more extensively in the coming cycle of the Earth when humanity will have become more subtle, for only those who are free of personal ties and who are already moving toward the spiritual kingdom can unrestrictedly build this relationship.

The spiritual and the divine kingdoms, like the kingdom of devas, evolve outside of the sphere of the law of karma. A large part of the inner Hierarchies of the planet, and even beyond, belong to these kingdoms. With the global transformations now underway, the spiritual kingdom will be able to flourish more freely on the surface of the Earth in a future cycle.

Up until now, only a minimal part of these sublime kingdoms and these Hierarchies has been revealed and perceived by humanity. Those who belong to the spiritual and divine kingdoms are no longer confined to the successive stages of initiation of human ascent; they have surpassed all this and live under broader laws.

The nonmaterial and impersonal attributes and tasks of the Hierarchies have been presented in an almost concrete way so that the human mind could grasp them and thus humanity of the surface of the Earth could consciously approach the spiritual level. However, as human beings broaden their mental horizons, after this preparatory stage they will be able to be in the presence of the essence of the Hierarchies without so many veils and personifications.

As long as humans cannot go beyond the material laws by themselves, the spiritual Hierarchies guide, protect and assist them. Once they are able to become uplifted, the Hierarchies shower gifts on them and make them their collaborators. This acting-together-with the Hierarchies dissolves the karma generated during the Earth's past and prepares the human kingdom for the freedom of the Cosmic Man.[8]

---

[8] **Cosmic Man.** Also called the Eighth Monad, Monadic Regent or Regent-Avatar, this is the deepest nucleus of the being. In some areas of mysticism it has also been called the Father.

Governance of the Law of Karma over the Planets

The law of karma carries out an equilibrating role in human beings and also throughout the universe of matter. Therefore, planets that exist in this sphere go through the stage of being governed by this law prior to entering a higher evolutionary state. Some planets have already fulfilled this stage and have acquired the knowledge that takes them beyond material boundaries. In this galaxy, the Earth, which is the planet with the heaviest karma, resists purification. The other planets are waiting for the Earth to advance so that all may share a better destiny.

The law of karma only governs the planets that are evolving on the physical, astral and mental levels. Other planets of the solar system, besides Earth, are also evolving on these levels, but they have developed in harmony with their spiritual goals; thus, although their karma exists, it is not so confining. Some planets in this same solar system interact intensely with laws other than the law of karma. These planets are in what could be called a state of vigil and they have no physical life.

When the time comes, there will be different pathways for human beings to transmigrate from this planet. When Jesus spoke of the many mansions of his Father's House, he might have been talking about this diversity of worlds, with their different forms of bringing about equilibrium.

The karma of planet Earth can be lightened by liberating the karma of the beings who inhabit its environs. As we have seen, this can be done in the human kingdom by continually making thoughts, feelings and actions more altruistic and less self-centered. This is easy to understand but not so easy to carry out. Nevertheless, it becomes more feasible when certain changes begin to take place, such as the awakening of one's right side consciousness, the implanting of the new genetic code in humanity and the alignment of the Earth with higher laws.

The law of karma is linked to the stage in which the Earth needed a great deal of external help in order to evolve. Had it not been for this help, the planet would have disintegrated. A planet that is still governed by the law of karma must balance its transgressions and since planetary progress is cyclical, the planet generally falls back into the same kind of error. On the other hand, the planets governed by the higher law of evolution follow an uninterrupted path of ascent because they do not relapse into former disharmonies.

Under the higher law of evolution, planets learn through experience. And with each lesson they overcome limitations and progress. On the other hand, the planets under the law of karma tend to repeat errors until the time of judgment, such as the one that the Earth is about to undergo. Times of judgment are needed to separate what gives way to involution from that which can be rescued for higher levels of existence.

The rhythm of the cosmos is vibrant; it does not yield to stagnation. An omnipresent Intelligence guides all that exists toward expansion, continually changing the configuration of the universes and adjusting them, and all beings in them, to the perfection of higher and broader laws.

A New Stage

If we were to consider the possibility of the life of this humanity becoming transformed according to a natural rhythm, we would find the chances to be minimal. Nevertheless, deep within each human being there pulses a certainty of *something* that is hovering, *something* that is not really perceived. No one knows how this *something* will be manifested, but it will renew the face of the Earth.

The planet is approaching a new stage of life. This is not a utopian idea; it is a perception based on truth. This new stage is not implanted through human merit, therefore we can say that a part of earthly life has already gone beyond karma.

Life beyond karma, so long awaited by all, will not come about through social, political or ideological movements. The new Earth is really a state of consciousness that already exists and that is awaiting the right time for it to surface.

Many will already find this new life within themselves as they recognize that the current civilization has fallen into complete decadence. Moreover, there are those who are treading the spiritual path inwardly, without being aware of it. The change will be a natural step that they will take without resisting or wavering. The new life has already silently permeated their being. Unperceived, it has taken root and radiates its energies.

Without any apparent reason, some people discover that they can no longer go on acting as they used to and thus they begin to free themselves from the law of karma. Without knowing how, they become receptive to higher things that they denied in the past. They perceive clarity, equilibrium and attunement with universal harmony flourishing within them. Their lives are absorbed into wider spheres. They are drawn toward something they had always aspired to, even though they never realized it. They overcome fear and transcend the perception as to what human beings can accomplish. A sacred Presence hovers over them.

Today we are at an important stage of this process and we have reached a delicate threshold. The physical substance of the Earth is turning into light to receive this new life. Therefore, transformations are occurring and an inner call is reverberating strongly once again. The flow of the great current will not be interrupted. The planet will enter the cosmic path that awaits it.

The next stage in the evolution of humanity began to be formed thousands of years ago. Now the time of its coming is assured and inevitable, despite appearances to the contrary. The vestments of the new humans have been woven on the inner levels of the planet and some have already learned how to wear them. This expansion will enable humans to express impartiality, neutrality and universality. They will be aware of the All and will treat fellow beings fraternally, whether they be in corporeal sheaths or already clothed in light, like the many extraterrestrial visitors who make themselves known in the skies. Humanity of the surface of the Earth will finally be able to radiate cristic love and to serve on various planets.

The new human beings will disengage themselves from projects for personal fulfillment and will strive to discover what can lead them to fullness as cosmic beings. They will seek to contact the inner essence that expands limits and helps them to transcend their human and sectarian aspects. Their lives will express service, love and will, for the sake of perpetuating the Light.

In the new stage, to find one's essence will be more than mere aspiration; it will be a living reality. There will be no ailments. Small disharmonies will be balanced through contact with healing energies radiated from natural and supernatural sources that will be well-known to humanity.

All will be aware of the task they came to fulfill on Earth as part of a broad Plan of Evolution. They will learn how to control the winds, the rains and the flow of the waters. They will cooperate consciously with interplanetary harmony, where higher laws govern the course of events and the structuring of forms.

The members of this new humanity will share mental unity, fruit of contact with intuitive levels of consciousness. The sense of separateness will give way to an awareness of the oneness of existence.

Human beings will then be consecrated as co-creators of the universe. This will come about because they will have transcended the law of karma and directed their free will to the choice of the divine. They will have recognized themselves as part of a sidereal world. They will be consciously living their own, ever more luminous, inner reality.

Then I saw a new heaven and a new earth;
the first heaven and the first earth had disappeared now,
and there was no longer any sea...
Then I heard a loud voice call from the throne,
"You see this city? Here God lives among men.
He will make his home among them;
they shall be his people,
and he will be their God;
His name is God-with-them.
He will wipe away all tears from their eyes;
there will be no more death
and no more mourning or sadness.
The world of the past has gone."

Revelation 21:1-4 [9]

---

[9] *The Jerusalem Bible, Reader's Edition* [Garden City, NY: Doubleday & Company, Inc. 1966].

About Trigueirinho and His Work

Jose Trigueirinho Netto (1931-2018) was born in Sao Paulo, Brazil. He lived in Europe for a number of years, where he maintained contact with individuals who were advanced on the spiritual path, including Paul Brunton.

In his own life he was an example of the teachings that he transmitted through his books and talks about the transcendence and elevation of the human being, the contact with the soul and with even more profound nuclei of the being, impersonal service, and the link with the Spiritual Hierarchies.

One of the fundamental elements of his work is to stimulate the expansion of human consciousness and to liberate it from the bonds that keep it imprisoned to material aspects of existence, both external and internal.

He was the Founder of the Community of Light Figueira (http://www.comunidadefigueira.org.br) and a Founder and member of the Board of Directors of the Fraternity International

Humanitarian Federation (www.fraterinternacional) as well as a Co-Founder of the Grace Mercy Order, an ecumenical Christian monastic order. He also was an active collaborator, instructor and spiritual protector of three other communities located in Uruguay, Argentina and Portugal.

In his last 30 years he lived in the Community of Light Figueira, in the interior of Minas Gerais, Brazil, a community that at present has approximately 300 residents and which is visited annually by thousands of collaborators who are members of a larger network of humanitarian services and of spiritual studies that was always guided and followed closely by Trigueirinho.

Thanks to his inestimable instruction and his love for the Kingdoms of Nature and as a result of the exemplary work that he himself implanted in the Figueira community, the Animal, Vegetable and Mineral Kingdoms are the recipients of loving treatment there.

Trigueirinho wrote over 80 books, published originally in Portuguese, with many of them translated into Spanish, English, French and German. He gave more than 3,000 talks that were recorded live and which are available in CD, with some available in DVD and pen drive. Approximately 100 of these recorded talks are available with English voice over at the website of the Shasti Association: http://www.shasti.org/instruction (drop down the menu tab titled "Trigueirinho Instruction" and then click on "MP3 audios").

The primary focus of the first phase of Trigueirinho's work was concerned with self-knowledge, prayer, instruction and spiritual transformation. Following this, he began to transmit information with respect to Universal Life and about the assistance that humanity has from its beginnings received by means of the Intra-terrestrial White Brotherhood which inhabits the Retreats and the Planetary Centers as well as through the Cosmic Brotherhood of the Universe. He provides information about the presence of the Spiritual Hierarchy on the planet and the advent of the new humanity.

His work also includes themes relating to: the need for humanity to balance the negative karmas that it has created in relation to the Kingdoms of Nature; the negative karmic burden that we carry from the history of slavery and the genocide of indigenous peoples; and the nature of spiritual work in groups. He also addresses issues of healing, a larger vision of astrology, the esoteric nature of symbols, sound and colors, and the divine feminine.

In his last eight years he analyzed with clarity and with the wisdom that always characterized him, the messages that the Divinity has been giving to the planet as a warning to humanity (available from www.mensajerosdivinos.org/en).

His work reveals a real comprehension of the significance of all the Kingdoms of Nature on our planet, the true spiritual task of the human being, its place in the universe and also its responsibility before Creation.

Finally, he clarifies the reasons for the crisis that today is devastating humanity, teaching how to avoid reacting negatively to an immanent natural catastrophe by contacting more subtle levels of consciousness, and opening perspectives for the beginning of a more luminous cycle for our race.

Books by Trigueirinho

(Books available in English have English title first)

Published by Editora Pensamento
Sao Paulo, Brazil

1987

NOSSA VIDA NOS SONHOS
OUR LIFE IN DREAMS

A ENERGIA DOS RAIOS EM NOSSA VIDA
THE ENERGY OF THE RAYS IN OUR LIVES

1988

DO IRREAL AO REAL
FROM THE UNREAL TO THE REAL

HORA DE CRESCER INTERIORMENTE
O Mito de Hércules Hoje
TIME FOR INNER GROWTH — *The Myth of Hercules Today*

A MORTE SEM MEDO E SEM CULPA
DEATH WITHOUT FEAR AND WITHOUT GUILT

CAMINHOS PARA A CURA INTERIOR
PATHS TO INNER HEALING

1989

ERKS – *Mundo Interno*
ERKS – *The Inner World*

Miz Tli Tlan – *Um Mundo que Desperta*
MIZ TLI TLAN – *A World that Awakens*

Aurora – **Essência Cósmica Curadora**
AURORA – *Cosmic Essence of Healing*

Signs of Contact
SINAIS DE CONTATO

O Novo Começo do Mundo
THE NEW BEGINNING OF THE WORLD

A Quinta Raça
THE FIFTH RACE

Padrões de conduta para a nova Humanidade
PATTERNS OF CONDUCT FOR THE NEW HUMANITY

Novos Sinais de Contato
NEW SIGNS OF CONTACT

Os Jardineiros do Espaço
THE SPACE GARDENERS

1990

A Busca da Síntese
THE SEARCH FOR SYNTHESIS

Noah's Vessel
A NAVE DE NOÉ

TEMPO DE RETIRO E TEMPO DE VIGÍLIA
A TIME OF RETREAT AND A TIME OF VIGIL

1991

PORTAS DO COSMOS
GATEWAYS OF THE COSMOS

ENCONTRO INTERNO – *A Consciência-Nave*
INNER ENCOUNTER – *The Consciousness Space Vessel*

A HORA DO RESGATE
THE TIME OF RESCUE

O LIVRO DOS SINAIS
THE BOOK OF SIGNS

MIRNA JAD – *Santuário Interior*
MIRNA JAD – *Inner Sanctuary*

AS CHAVES DE OURO
THE GOLDEN KEYS

1992

DAS LUTAS À PAZ
FROM STRUGGLE TO PEACE

A MORADA DOS ELISÍOS THE ELYSIAN DWELLING PLACE

HORA DE CURAR – *A Existência Oculta*
TIME FOR HEALING – *The Occult Existence*

O RESSURGIMENTO DE FÁTIMA LIS
THE RESURGENCE OF FATIMA LIS

História Escrita nos Espelhos
Princípios de Comunicação Cósmic
HISTORY WRITTEN IN THE MIRRORS -
Principles of Cosmic Communication

Passos Atuais
STEPS FOR NOW

Viagem por Mundos Sutis
TRAVEL THROUGH SUBTLE WORLDS

Segredos Desvelados – *Iberah e Anu Tea*
UNVEILED SECRETS – *Iberah and Anu Tea*

A Criação – *Nos Caminhos da Energia*
CREATION – *On the Paths of Energy*

The Mystery of the Cross In the Present Planetary Transition
O MISTÉRIO DA CRUZ NA ATUAL TRANSIÇÃO PLANETÁRIA

O Nascimento da Humanidade Futura
THE BIRTH OF THE FUTURE HUMANITY

1993

Aos Que Despertam
TO THOSE WHO AWAKEN

Paz Interna em Tempos Críticos
INNER PEACE IN CRITICAL TIMES

A Formação de Curadores
THE FORMATION OF HEALERS

Profecias aos Que Não Temem Dizer Sim
PROPHECIES FOR THOSE WHO ARE NOT AFRAID TO SAY YES

THE VOICE OF AMHAJ
A VOZ DE AMHAJ

O VISITANTE – O CAMINHO PARA ANU TEA
THE VISITOR – *The Way to Anu Tea*

A CURA DA HUMANIDADE
THE HEALING OF HUMANITY

OS NÚMEROS E A VIDAS – *Uma Nova Compreensão da Simbologia Oculta nos Números*
NUMBERS AND LIFE – *A New Understanding of Occult Symbolism in Numbers*

NISKALKAT – *Uma Mensagem para os Tempos de Emergência*
NISKALKAT – *A Message for Times of Emergency*

ENCONTROS COM A PAZ
ENCOUNTERS WITH PEACE

NOVOS ORÁCULOS
NEW ORACLES

UM NOVO IMPULSO ASTROLÓGICO
A NEW ASTROLOGICAL IMPULSE

1994

BASES DO MUNDO ARDENTE – *Indicações para Contato com os Mundos suprafíscicos*
BASES OF THE FIERY WORLD – *Indications for Contacts with Supraphysical Worlds*

CONTATOS COM UM MONASTÉRIO INTERATERRENO
CONTACTS WITH AN INTRATERRESTRIAL MONASTERY

Os oceanos têm Ouvidos
OCEANS HAVE EARS

A Trajetória do Fogo
THE PATH OF FIRE

Glossário Esotérico
ESOTERIC LEXICON

1995

The Light Within You
A LUZ DENTRO DE TI

1996

Doorway to a Kingdom
PORTAL PARA UM REINO

Beyond Karma
ALÉM DO CARMA

1997

We Are Not Alone
NÃO ESTAMOS SÓS

Winds of the spirit
VENTOS DO ESPÍRITO

Finding the Temple
O ENCONTRO DO TEMPLO

There is Peace
A PAZ EXISTE

1998

Path Without Shadows
CAMINHO SEM SOMBRAS

Mensagens para Uma Vida de Harmonia
MESSAGES FOR A LIFE OF HARMONY

1999

Toque Divino
THE DIVINE TOUCH

Coleção Pedaços de Céu
  BITS FROM HEAVEN COLLECTION
- **Aromas do Espaço**
  AROMAS FROM SPACE
- **Nova Vida Bate à Porta**
  A NEW LIFE AWAITS YOU
- **Mais Luz No Horizonte**
  MORE LIGHT ON THE HORIZON
- **O Campanário Cósmico**
  THE COSMIC CAMPANILE
- **Nada Nos Falta**
  WE LACK NOTHING
- **Sagrados Mistérios**
  SACRED MYSTERIES
- **Ilhas de Salvação**
  ISLANDS OF SALVATION

2002

Calling Humanity
  UM CHAMADO ESPECIAL

2004

És Viajante Cósmico
YOU ARE A COSMIC WAYFARER

Impulsos
IMPULSES

2005

Pensamentos para Todo o Ano
THOUGHTS FOR THE WHOLE YEAR

2006

Trabalho Espiritual com a Mente
SPIRITUAL WORK WITH THE MIND

Published by Editora Irdin
Carmo da Cachoeira, Minas Gerais, Brazil

2009

Signs of Blavatsky – *An Unusual Encounter for the Present Time*
SINAIS DE BLAVATSKY – *Um Inusitado Encontro nos Dias de Hoje*

2012

Consciências e Hierarquias
CONSCIOUSNESSES AND HIERARCHIES

2015

Mensagens Reunidas
COLLECTED MESSAGES

Mensagens para Sua Tranformaçã
MESSAGES FOR YOUR TRANSFORMATION

2017

Páginas de Amor e Compreensão
PAGES OF LOVE AND COMPREHENSION

2018

Novos Tempos: Nova Postura
NEW TIMES: NEW ATTITUDE

2020

Versos Livres
OBRA PÓSTUMA

Trigueirinho's works are published by:

Associação Irdin Editora – www.irdin.org.br (selected titles of books in English, Spanish and Portuguese and CDs in several languages), Carmo da Cachoeira, MG, Brazil.

Editora Pensamento – www.pensamento-cultrix.com.br (titles in Portuguese), São Paulo, SP, Brazil

Editorial Kier – www.kier.com.ar (selected titles in Spanish), Buenos Aires, Argentina.

Lichtwelle-Verlag – www.lichtwelle-verlag.ch (selected titles in Spanish and German), Zurich, Switzerland.

Shasti Association – www.shasti.org (selected titles in English), Mount Shasta, CA, USA

Lectures of Trigueirinho with Simultaneous English Translation

During over thirty years as Founder of the Figueira Community of Light, Trigueirinho gave bi-weekly lectures (called 'parthilha's or 'sharings') that were recorded live. Audience members were invited to submit questions to him which were placed in a small box and brought to him by an attendant. Arriving early, Trigueirinho sat at the lectern, reading through and taking notes on the audience questions. Thus, his lectures often began with the phrase "someone has asked a question…." After addressing some of these questions, he continued with the theme chosen for the day.

Approximately 70 of these 'sharings' were later dubbed with English translations. His voice or the translators can be augmented or diminished by adjusting the right-left balance of the recording.

To access these audio recordings go to: www.shasti.org/instruction, then drop down the menu tab titled "Trigueirinho Instruction" and then click on "MP3 audios."

A Book to Be Written
A New Viewpoint of the Monad
Alopathic and Homeopathic Medicine
An Esoteric Dimension of Power
An Overview of Current Life
Angels and Humanity – 1
Angels and Humanity – 2
Angels and Humanity – 3
Angels and Humanity – 4
Bases of the Fiery World
Beyond Fire by Friction
Beyond Imperfection
Causal Body
Colors in Healing and the Formation of Our Light Vessel
Deep Healing
From the Human Kingdom to the Spiritual Kingdom
Getting through Today's Critical Times
Harmonization and Androgyny
How One Begins to Perceive One's Inner Self
How to Understand the Planetary Disasters
Human Trials | The Trials of the Soul
Information on the New Earth and the New Humanity
Inner and Outer Figueira
Instruction: a Step beyond Teaching
Liberating and Healing through Colors
Life in Cosmic Signs
New Supraterrestrial Pathways – 1
New Supraterrestrial Pathways – 2
New Supraterrestrial Pathways – 3
New Supraterrestrial Pathways – 4
Niskalkat
Noah's Vessel
On Vitality
Our Response to the Cosmos – 1
Our Response to the Cosmos – 2
Our Response to the Cosmos – 3
Our Response to the Cosmos – 4
Our Response to the Cosmos – 5
Our Response to the Cosmos – 6
Preparation for the Path of Initiation
Reflections on Illusion and Rescue
Reflections on Inner Attunement
Seeds of Inner Transformation
Seeking to Understand the Self

Several Levels of Spiritual Reading
Special Paths and the Path of the Majority
Spiritual Entities and Hierarchies
Spiritual Trials
Strengthening the Bases for the New Cycles
Subtle Bodies and Templing
Supraterrestrial Pathways – 1
Supraterrestrial Pathways – 2
Supraterrestrial Pathways – 3
Supraterrestrial Pathways – 4
Syntheses, Struggles and New Instructions
Taking Charge of One's Process of Dying – 1
Taking Charge of One's Process of Dying – 2
Taking Charge of One's Process of Dying – 3
The Art of Living in Current Times
The Cosmic Signs Reveal the Teaching – 1
The Cosmic Signs Reveal the Teaching – 2
The Desert
The Earth – Degeneration and Deliverance
The Era of the Gigantic Wave
The Importance of Self-Control in Epidemics
  and Other Risk Situations
The Light That Permeates Matter
The Mystery of the Cross in the Present
  Planetary Transition
The Doorways of the Planet – 1
The Doorways of the Planet – 2
The Doorways of the Planet – 3
The Doorways of the Planet – 4
The Doorways of the Planet – 5
The Days of Tomorrow
The Heart, the Ego and the Personality
The New Life That is Emerging
The Plan of Evolution and Us
The Practical Mystic
The Seventh Ray and the Devas
The Spark from the Divine Level
The Transmutation of the Logos of the Earth
The Voice of Amhaj
To Be Universal – Part 1
To Be Universal – Part 2

To Medical Doctors and Therapists
To Those Who Pray – 1
To Those Who Pray – 2
Towards Self Consecration
We are Part of the Cosmos
Working Spiritually with One's Mind
Working with the Feminine Polarity
Working with the Rays

www.ingramcontent.com/pod-product-compliance
Lightning Source LLC
Chambersburg PA
CBHW030338100526
44592CB00010B/730